The Crisis of Parliamentary Democracy

Studies in Contemporary German Social Thought
Thomas McCarthy, General Editor

The Crisis of Parliamentary Democracy

Carl Schmitt
translated by Ellen Kennedy

The MIT Press, Cambridge, Massachusetts, and London, England

First MIT Press paperback edition, 1988

This book was originally published as *Die geistesgeschichtliche Lage des heutigen Parlamentarismus*, © 1923, 1926 by Duncker & Humblot, Berlin. The review by Richard Thoma was originally published in the *Archiv für Sozialwissenschaft und Sozialpolitik* 53 (1925), 215–217.

This book was set in Baskerville by The MIT Press Computergraphics Department and was printed and bound in the United States of America.

Library of Congress Cataloging-in-Publication Data

Schmitt, Carl, 1888–
   The crisis of parliamentary democracy.

   (Studies in contemporary German social thought)
Translation of: Die geistesgeschichtliche Lage des heutigen Parlamentarismus.
   Bibliography: p.
   Includes index.
   1. Legislative bodies. 2. Parliamentary practice.
I. Title. II. Series.
JF511.S313   1985   328'.3   85-19908
ISBN 0-262-19240-3 (hardcover)
    0-262-69126-4 (paperback)

Contents

Series Editor's Foreword

At the time of his death in April 1985 Carl Schmitt was generally acknowledged to be one of the most influential political thinkers of twentieth-century Germany. He was almost certainly the most controversial. A leading legal scholar of Weimar Germany, he entered public life as a constitutional adviser to the government during the last years of the Republic, then shifted his allegiance to the National Socialist regime after Hitler's rise to power. Schmitt's notoriety stems from this latter phase of his career; but his reputation as a thinker rests primarily on a number of brilliant, if somewhat idiosyncratic and apparently nihilistic, political-theoretical works of the Weimar period. We have decided to include translations of three of Schmitt's major writings from this period—*Political Romanticism* (1919), *Political Theology* (1922), and *The Crisis of Parliamentary Democracy* (1923)—in this series.

Why translate Schmitt, a thinker whose basic problems and assumptions took shape more than fifty years ago in the collapse of the nineteenth-century social order and whose own brief public life led him to become one of the most visible academic supporters and intellectual ornaments of the new National Socialist order? There are a number of reasons. First, Schmitt's incisive analyses of the fundamental problems of political theory—the nature of sovereignty, the legitimacy of the state, the basis of constitutionality and its relation to the rights and obligations of the individual, the purpose and limits of political power—mark him as one of the most original and powerful thinkers in this century to have struggled with the problems of Machiavelli, Hobbes, Locke, Rousseau, and Kant. Schmitt's work belongs integrally to the continuing dialogue of Western political thought that extends from Plato and Aristotle to the present. Second, Schmitt's contributions to the debate over political leadership in mass democracies, his unerring sense for the fundamental problems of modern politics, and his radical and systematic critique of the ideas and institutions of liberal democracy—an attack that has never been adequately answered—distinguish him as one of the most important figures in the theory of modern politics. Finally, the contemporary world shows many resemblances with the Schmittian political cosmos in which the conditions for politics-as-usual rarely obtain. It is marked not only by global economic, environmental, and military dangers that threaten existing social orders, but also by a tendency to theologize political conflicts, to transform domestic and international adversaries into enemies who represent the forces of evil. It is in many important respects that political world of exceptions, emergencies, and crises to which Schmitt, more than any other thinker of our time, devoted his considerable energies.

I would like to thank George Schwab and Guy Oakes for their invaluable assistance in arranging this series of Schmitt translations.

Thomas McCarthy
Northwestern University

A Note on the Text and Translation

This translation is based on the 1926 edition of *Die geistesgeschichtliche Lage des heutigen Parlamentarismus*. This second edition was enlarged by the inclusion of Schmitt's reply to Richard Thoma's 1925 review as a preface. I have retained the order of parts as Carl Schmitt set them out in the German text, although the addition of Thoma's "On the Ideology of Parliamentarism," and most of the notes, the index, and the bibiliography are new.

Carl Schmitt's style is remarkably clear and free of the convolutions that often burden academic German, but the title already contains a work notoriously difficult to render adequately in English: *geistesgeschichtliche*. I have usually translated this and its variants as "intellectual," or "intellectual-historical" if this is not awkward; but readers should be aware that the root word, *Geist*, has complex meanings in the original German, mixing "moral" and "spiritual" with our "intellectual" or "mind." Certain other German words and phrases have been left as terms of art—*Rechtsstaat*, for example—on the suggestion of someone who long struggled with the translation of Hegel into English. Carl Schmitt is certainly not as difficult to translate, but I still found this a sound rule to follow. Throughout this edition all works, including the one by Schmitt translated here, are referred to by their original titles.

I chose as an English title *The Crisis of Parliamentary Democracy*; this departs from a literal translation of Schmitt's original but nevertheless seems to me to capture its spirit. There is a slight precedent for this title in the English edition of a text to which Schmitt refers: Moritz Julius Bonn's *Die Auflösung der europäischen Demokratie* (1925), which in English became *The Crisis of European Democracy*. German political theorists at this time in the Weimar Republic were understandably prone to think in terms of crises of the state and of public values. I hope that in underlining this connection between Carl Schmitt's text and those of his contemporaries I have made it easier to hear Schmitt's voice as one among many in the same conversation.

Most of the work on this edition was done while I was a Fellow of the Alexander-von-Humboldt Stiftung; no one could ask for a more understanding and humane institutional sponsor, and it is a pleasure to thank the Humboldt Stiftung here for their generous support in 1981–1982. Those years were spent as a guest in the Seminar für wissenschaftliche Politik at the University of Freiburg, and I owe a special debt of thanks to its director, Professor Wilhelm Hennis. He was not only a vigorous and challenging colleague but a patient and tactful friend as well. Professor Heinrich Winkler extended the hospitality of the Historisches Seminar to me during my time in Freiburg, and I was particularly fortunate to be able to attend his seminars on the Weimar Republic and German historiography.

Professor Carl Schmitt allowed me to examine papers related to the origins of the text and its publication. I am grateful to him for his encouragement as I undertook the preparation of his *Parlamentarismus* for an English-speaking audience and for acting as a voice from the Weimar Republic as I tried to think through the intention of his text. Herr Ernst Thamm of Duncker & Humblot provided valuable information about the firm's archival holdings. Professors Joseph Bendersky, Thomas McCarthy, and George Schwab each commented

Note on the Text and Translation

on earlier drafts of the introduction and parts of the translation. The Bundesarchiv, Koblenz, and the Bundesarchiv-Militär Archiv, Freiburg, allowed me to use their holdings, as did the Institut für Zeitgeschichte, Munich, and the Wiener Library, London. This task would have been impossible without the wealth of contemporary political and legal holdings which I found in the University of Freiburg. The librarians in the Universitätsbibliothek were always efficient, and helpful whenever possible. And they were also—disproving an old and undeserved assumption about the Germans—unfailingly good-humored and cheerful. Hours of dictation in English were transcribed by Michaela Karl in the Seminar für wissenschaftliche Politik with equal good cheer and accuracy. In the last stages of preparing the manuscript the Institute for Social Sciences at the University of York provided assistance with the typing.

To all these persons and institutions, my thanks. Only the errors and mistakes are mine alone.

Ellen Kennedy
The University of York, England

Introduction: Carl Schmitt's *Parlamentarismus* in Its Historical Context

Ellen Kennedy

Le principe détermine les formes; les formes révélert le principe.
—Guizot (1851)

In der Tat steht und fällt eine Institution nicht mit ihrer Ideologie, sondern mit dem, was Carl Schmitt selbst als ihre Vitalität, Substanz, Kraft bezeichnet.
—Rudolf Smend (1928)

The most common reading of Carl Schmitt's *Die geistesgeschichtliche Lage des heutigen Parlamentarismus* starts from the assumption that it was a text "welcome to the broad spectrum of antiparliamentary prejudices in the Weimar Republic," which by its method as much as its content pushed the polarities of the Weimar constitution further apart. According to this interpretation, Schmitt was "the theorist for the resentments of a generation" whose critique of parliamentary democracy undermined the foundations of the first German republic by calling into question one of its central political institutions, the Reichstag. Little has changed in that view since 1923. Sixty years later, Schmitt's *Parlamentarismus* was described as a text of "terrible relevance," one to be read as a warning about "where one ends up if the temptations of antiparliamentarism are once given in to." There is only one alternative to parliamentarism, Christian Graf von Krockow wrote in late 1983: "If formal majorities no longer have the final word . . . then the slogan of the hour must be—dictatorship."[1]

This view is remarkable, not because it is unusual, but because the same question and argument had already been advanced in Richard Thoma's 1925 review of Schmitt's essay.[2] Eight years before Adolf Hitler's appointment as *Reichskanzler* ended democracy in Germany, Thoma charged Schmitt with a sympathy for the irrational in politics and a barely concealed preference for a dictatorship allied with the Catholic Church as the solution to Germany's political problems. Despite Schmitt's rejection of this charge in his reply to Thoma, the view that his critique of parliamentary government was in fact a prelude to dictatorship has nevertheless persisted. To understand why this is so, and to reach a judgment about the validity of this interpretation, Schmitt's *Parlamentarismus* must first be seen in its historical and intellectual context.

The context of *Parlamentarismus*

In the first years of the Weimar Republic Carl Schmitt was closely identified with political Catholicism. *Römischer Katholizismus und politische Form* (1923, 1925) and Schmitt's close contact with Catholic political and intellectual circles had made him by 1926 the leading exponent of the Catholic view among German jurists,[3] and his views also had a wider appeal in Europe. One of the most influential supporters of his analysis of parliamentarism and democracy was Karl Muth, editor of the Catholic journal *Hochland*. Returning from France in spring 1926, Muth wrote to Schmitt: "In Paris I had many opportunities to speak with French people about you. There is a very lively interest in your work, and one afternoon at Jacques Maritain's, I happened to meet the translator of your *Politische Romantik*, Monsieur Linn. I gave your article from the June issue, 'On the Contradiction between Modern Mass Democracy and Parliamentarism,' to Georges Goyan, among others, who expressed much interest."[4]

Parlamentarismus had first appeared in 1923 in the University of Bonn Law Faculty's festschrift for Ernst Zitelmann.[5] Schmitt approached the publishers Duncker & Humblot about a second edition of his essay the following year, and a contract was signed in June. But before Duncker & Humblot were prepared to issue the second edition, Richard Thoma's review appeared. In early 1926 Schmitt wrote to Karl Muth, suggesting that *Hochland* publish his reply, and Muth agreed.[6] When the manuscript was submitted to Ludwig Feuchtwanger, Schmitt's editor at Duncker & Humblot, Schmitt asked that the reply be included as a preface.[7] Neither Muth nor Feuchtwanger objected, and Schmitt's reply to Thoma appeared in both *Hochland* and the second edition of his *Parlamentarismus* in 1926.

Some indication of how Schmitt (and his editor) viewed the essay is given in the correspondence between them on its title and the publisher's original proposal for a second edition. In reply to Schmitt's urging that a new edition appear in 1925, Feuchtwanger expressed doubt that the market was favorable: "No one buys a book today that is not directly and closely connected to some concrete existential purpose, such as passing an examination, or which serves some professional requirements, etc., *or* which is a sensation. . . ." As an alternative, Feuchtwanger offered to publish Schmitt's *Parlamentarismus* in 1926: "Next year we are reissuing some of our out-of-print brochures which are the most important and most frequently asked for, in identical form: Max Weber, *Politik als Beruf*; Simmel, *Der Konflikt der modernen Kultur*; Bendixen (the late Hamburg Bank director), *Das Wesen des Gelds*; Becher (now professor of philosophy), *Metaphysik und Naturwissenschaft*; and lastly, your *Parlamentarismus*." He suggested that the five might appear with a covering title page identifying them as "Beiträge zur Kulturwissenschaft"; they were in any case "united by their intellectual superiority."[8] When Schmitt's manuscript had been submitted, Feuchtwanger wrote back on May 6, 1926, confirming that it would be set and printed with the others in the summer.

Schmitt had agreed to Feuchtwanger's suggestion in late 1925 that the title be changed to *Die* moralische *Lage des heutigen Parlamentarismus* on condition that this should not delay the book's appearance.[9] Feuchtwanger's preference for *moral* instead of *intellectual-historical* was spelled out in a letter to Schmitt on May 14, 1926: "In spite of being well-worn, *moral* says more in this connection than *intellectual* and almost anticipates the result. The word allows the endangered prestige of contemporary parliamentarism to shine through already. If we speak about the 'moral' situation of a public institution—and that as a title, too—then where the journey takes us is very clearly said. *geistesgeschichtlich* [intellectual-historical] is too thin, and as you say, it has been compromised by literary historians."[10]

Schmitt's *Parlamentarismus* belongs to an early phase of his work in which he was preoccupied with a cultural critique of modern society and the history of political ideas, yet turning points on the way to "decisionism" can already be seen in this essay. The series of books appearing between 1919 and 1926 allows these to be traced with some specificity. There was, first of all, Schmitt's critique of political romanticism as an *ewige Gespräch* (endless conversation) in his *Politische Romantik* (1919), a study of the political ideas of the German romantics and the career of Adam Müller, which became a standard work on the subject.[11] This was followed by *Die Diktatur* (1921), which expanded the work Schmitt had done during the First World War on the concepts of "a state of siege" and "emergency" in a history of the political theory of dictatorship in modern Europe.[12] His *Politische Theologie* (1922) took up aspects of both earlier works and contained an indictment of the weakness of the bourgeoisie whose political representation Schmitt found in liberals and liberalism.[13] Just as the romantic avoids taking decisions, so too the liberal; faced with the question, "Christ or Barabbas, the liberal answers with a motion to adjourn the meeting or set up an investigative committee."[14] An essay on the institution most characteristic of liberalism, parliament, was thus a logical development in Schmitt's thought. So too were the reply to Thoma[15] and the treatise on the plebiscitary provisions of the Weimar constitution, *Volksentscheid und Volksbegehren* (1926, 1927).[16]

To understand why this relatively slim volume has had such a persistently controversial place in German thought during this century, we must return to his contemporaries' view of it and the exchange between Carl Schmitt and Richard Thoma, which Rudolf Smend called "the most exciting and instructive controversy in state theory in recent years."[17]

Schmitt's thesis and Thoma's critique

Richard Thoma raised two objections to Schmitt's view of parliamentarism. First, that it was purely ideological, dealing only with the political theory of parliament as an institution and liberalism as a doctrine; and second, that Carl Schmitt had mistaken the ideological foundations of contemporary parliamentarism in Germany. These were not, as Schmitt asserted, the classical texts of liberal political thought in England and France, but the political ideas of the Weimar Republic and its constitutional authors—Max Weber, Friedrich Naumann, and Hugo Preuss.[18] Schmitt had stated that his intention was to examine why parliament had been "the *ultimum sapientiae* for many generations [of Europeans]," and to understand that, he maintained, it was necessary to look at "the ultimate core of the institution of modern parliament" and the intellectual foundations of parliamentarism itself.[19] These cannot be technical or pragmatic justifications, such as Thoma advanced; and Schmitt specifically refused to accept the rationale that because there really is no better alternative (and there are many worse ones) to parliamentary government, there can be no discussion of its principles. Although he certainly knew the work of Naumann, Preuss, and Weber, Schmitt insisted that they provided no new principled arguments for parliamentarism; rather, their views assume the "classical" theories of liberalism. If parliamentarism is to be understood correctly in its historical circumstances, attention must first be given to its political philosophy—to the idea of parliament first, then to its function. These, Schmitt argued, were most cogently set out by Locke, Bentham, Burke, and Mill in England and by Guizot in France.

The first edition of Schmitt's essay on parliamentarism was completed before the onset of the most severe crisis of early Weimar, in the autumn and winter of 1923, but it had been written during and after the period of serious disturbances in Germany that persisted from November 1918. Nevertheless, the text makes no direct reference to these events. Rather, the first edition concentrated on the essence of parliamentarism as it can be understood from the classic theories and modern European political experience, especially in the nineteenth century. The argument, which Thoma criticized in his review two years later, was that the essence of parliamentarism is openness and discussion, because these are recognized in liberal political philosophy as the means of political reason: One believed that naked power and force—for liberal, *Rechtsstaat* thinking, an evil in itself, 'the way of beasts,' as Locke said—could be overcome "through openness and discussion alone, and the victory of right over might achieved."[20] But new political doctrines and movements now cast doubt on the vitality of belief in these principles. Schmitt contended further that political experience under the Weimar constitution revealed these ideas, and with them parliament as a political institution, as outdated. The crisis of contemporary parliamentarism in Germany had become so acute, he replied to Thoma in 1926, because "the development of modern mass democracy has made public discussion an empty formality."[21] Thoma had agreed with Schmitt that the principles he identified with parliamentarism—openness and discussion—were "outdated"; their disagreement arose from Schmitt's assertion that this also made parliamentary government "outdated." Schmitt's contention was based ultimately on a claim about the logic of propositions in the justification of political choice and action, and on Harold Laski's definition of parliament as "government by discussion."[22] The first of these will be considered in greater detail below; the second, borrowed from contemporary English political thought, made strong claims for the efficacy of a liberal theory of politics. According to Schmitt's interpretation, discussion forces those in authority to declare their positions and debate alternatives openly. In the liberal system, a free press and freedom of opinion provide the public with access to information independent of what the authorities say, so that it knows what is being done and for what reasons. By these means, citizens control the use of power. Furthermore, liberal theory assumes that discussion produces a dialectic of opinions and ideas, from which the general will, or public good, emerges. That parliamentarism creates a will that is general (and not merely, as Rousseau says, "the will of all") is, in Carl Schmitt's interpretation, its ultimate claim to legitimacy.

Because discussion is central to liberalism, a series of familiar institutional structures has been developed to protect it: checks and balances, the division of powers, and a catalogue of civil rights that is common to most liberal democracies. These are hindrances to the abuse of political power, but their underlying justification, Schmitt claims, derives from "a consistent, comprehensive metaphysical system."[23] The necessity for discussion is no less epistemological than it is political; in liberalism, the search for truth goes on as a conversation from which force is absent and where reason and persuasion prevail. Liberal political theory thus depends on an assumption that political conflict can be transformed into a matter of opinion; the better informed and more "enlightened" the public is, the closer it will come to the truth, and on this reading, parliament becomes the greatest force for the political education not only of leaders but also of the public. Parliament's job, performed through debate and questioning, is to sort out conflicting opinions and evidence, so that parliamentary government can govern not just by dint of holding power or through authority but because it comes closest to the truth. Accordingly the constituents of a theory of responsible and accountable government, in the liberal view, are organized around securing a dialectic of opinion; question time in parliament, legislative committees, press scrutiny, and the ultimate sanction of the ballot box all serve that end.

Just how radical Carl Schmitt's analysis of parliamentarism was becomes apparent in his second chapter, "The Principles of Parliamentarism." Thoma's critique of this interpretation of liberalism was only an academic point in the controversy Schmitt's essay caused after 1923.[24] More sustained disagreement was based on the immediate question of parliamentarism in the Weimar Republic, and specifically on the supposed implications of Schmitt's argument for an interpretation of the executive and legislative in the constitution. One recent commentator on Schmitt's political thought has written that the essay on parliamentarism was motivated by an attempt to discover "whether the constitution was a consistent document."[25] According to Schmitt's interpretation as it developed between 1923 and 1926 (between the first and second editions of *Parlamentarismus*), it was not. The Weimar constitution contained two principles, one liberal and the other democratic. During these years Schmitt began to identify these two principles with the Reichstag and the Reichspräsident, respectively. This development in Schmitt's political thought is as important for understanding why his views on parliamentary government were so controversial as are Schmitt's declared intentions between 1923 and 1926.

Parliament and democracy after the German revolution: Hugo Preuss and Max Weber

The German Reich proclaimed in article 1 of the Weimar constitution was a democracy and a republic.[26] But Thoma's view that "with article 1, section 2, the nation is already thought—that is, the Germans as such, not differentiated in this way or that"[27]—conceals the principal constitutional problem that confronted its authors: "The Weimar Republic was neither the necessary result of an organic political development nor the achievement of a spontaneous, historically self-legitimating revolution."[28] There were no "Germans as such" in 1918, and the radically different views of Germany's political future during the winter of 1918–1919 structured the possibilities for a new constitution. In

Introduction

the document that was finally agreed upon, a liberal view advanced by Weber and Preuss triumphed over political ideas advocated by the forces these men most feared. With the calling of a National Assembly and its acceptance of a *bürgerliche Rechtsstaat* as the German state form, German liberals blocked the permanent institution of a *verkehrter Obrigkeitsstaat*—a socialist state on the model of the Soviet Union that would have transformed German society and excluded the German bourgeoisie from political and economic participation.

The single most important hand in drafting the Weimar constitution was undoubtedly Hugo Preuss, then Staatssekretär in the Reich Interior Ministry. In November 1918 Preuss argued that if the social and political goals of the Rätebewegung and the radical left represented by the Independent Socialists (later the German Communist party) were realized, then the German state would be constituted in the shadow of repression that would "in a very short time lead to Bolshevist terror."[29] Only two days after Philipp Scheidemann proclaimed the republic to a crowd in the front of the Reichstag, Preuss wrote in the *Berliner Tageblatt* that the authoritarian state had "in no way been replaced by a popular state [*Volksstaat*], but by a reversed authoritarian state [*umgedrehter Obrigkeitsstaat*]."[30] For him the question was clear; under the Kaiser, democratization on Western lines had been blocked: "Do we now want to copy bolshevism, the reverse side of the old czarism?" There were only two alternatives: "Either Wilson or Lenin, either the democracy that developed out of the French and American revolutions or the brutal form of Russian fanaticism. One must choose."[31]

In these circumstances, Preuss believed that a democratically elected National Assembly should decide Germany's future: "If there is not a solution to the German constitutional question that assumes the equality of all members of the nation [*Volksgenossen*] in a politically democratic organization, then there is no other way out than lawless force and with it the complete destruction of economic life."[32]

In late November 1918 the temporary government (*Rat der Volksbeauftragten*) under the Social Democrat (and later first president of the republic) Friedrich Ebert entrusted the draft of a new constitution to Preuss. His "Denkschrift zum Entwurf des allgemeinen Teils der Reichsverfassung" was submitted on January 3, 1919, and published in the *Reichsanzeiger* on January 20.[33] Preuss's plan for a democratic republic was guided by the thought that the new German Reich must be the result of "the national self-consciousness of a self-organizing people." In contrast to Bismarck's unification of the German states under Prussian hegemony in 1871, this Reich should be "a unified national state founded on the free self-determination of the whole people."[34] Yet the essentially democratic idea that the people themselves were the constitution-giving power in Germany did not resolve the question of how Germany should be governed and what form the concept of democracy in the state and German politics should take. In the end, a mixed constitution was adopted, one that stitched together elements of direct and indirect democracy and moderated the people's democratic power through liberal institutions.

Views similar to Preuss's were also advanced by Max Weber during the winter of 1918–1919. Like Preuss, Weber was concerned to forestall the exclusion of the German middle classes from political participation by radical left-wing forces he thought immature and dangerous. Again, like Preuss, Weber emphasized the importance of German unity in defeat and in the face of severe Allied economic pressure. Against the "revolutionary carnival" (*Revolutionskarnaval*), Weber's political theory held up an ideal of rational and competent political leadership.[35]

Weber's work during the last years of the war shows that he was anxious to check the means to caesaristic power in Germany, which the military had already begun to make use of and which he thought would become increasingly dangerous. In a series of articles published in the *Frankfurter Zeitung* during summer 1918, but written in the winter before, Weber argued that demagoguery was the greatest danger in democratic states. In modern mass democracy, it is a potential in the organization of political power around the democratic leader's appeal to the voters that could easily become caesaristic: "The importance of active mass democratization is that the political leader no longer becomes a candidate because he is esteemed within a circle of political notables and then, as a result of his work in parliament, becomes the leader. Rather, he wins his political power through mass-demagogic means and holds it on the basis of the trust and confidence of the masses."[36] Because of the danger of caesarism he thought it implied, Weber at that time opposed direct election of many state offices: "Every kind of direct election of the highest authorities, and in fact every kind of political power that depends on the trust of the masses [and] not parliament . . . is on the way toward this 'pure' form of caesaristic acclamation."[37] Caesaristic leaders come to power either through the military (Napoleon I) or by direct appeal to the people in plebiscites (Napoleon III). Both, Weber argued, are fundamental contradictions of the parliamentary principle.[38]

A year later Weber's views had changed. In "Deutschlands künftige Staatsform," he argued for a "plebiscitary Reichspräsident" with power to appeal directly to the people in case of a governmental deadlock, and he saw referenda as a means to resolve conflicts between the federal and unitary agencies of the state.[39] Three months after "Deutschlands künftige Staatsform" appeared and after Friedrich Ebert had been elected as the first Reichspräsident by the National Assembly in Weimar, Weber wrote that "future Reichspräsident(s) must be directly elected by the people."[40] Although most of his misgivings about popular election seemed to have been assuaged, an element of Weber's earlier fears remained. Presidential power should be balanced by parliamentary power and defined in such a way that it could be used only "in temporarily insoluble crises (through a suspensive veto and the appointment of bureaucratic ministers). But one must give him independent ground under his feet through popular election. Otherwise the whole Reich structure will wobble in a parliamentary crisis—and with at least four or five parties, these will not be infrequent."[41]

The debate on parliamentarism in early Weimar

For German liberals in 1919 two systems of parliamentarism presented themselves as models—England and France. Each received considerable attention in Max Weber's political writings, along with the American presidential system; and before drafting his design of the new constitution, Hugo Preuss read Robert Redslob's and Robert Piloty's works on parliamentary governments in Europe and Wilhelm Hasbach's study of cabinet government.[42] Both Weber and Preuss shared Redslob's view that English parliamentarism was the "true" or, in Weber's words, the "real" form of parliamentarism.[43] But the English model alone was not adequate to German circumstances in 1918–1919, nor could it be so simply applied. Only a very small circle of Germans had concerned themselves with the complex of questions implied in democracy, and in broad sections of society there was open hostility to parliamentarism and to democracy in any form. When German politicians were forced in the autumn of 1918 to improvise a parliamentary system, Thomas Mann retorted, "I want the monarchy, I want a passionately independent government, because only it offers protection for freedom in the intellectual as well as the economic sphere. . . . I don't want this parliament and party business that will sour the whole life of the nation with its politics. . . . I don't want politics. I want competence, order, and decency."[45] Neither German political culture nor the circumstances in which the monarchy came to an end and in which governments of the first Weimar years had to govern strengthened the constitution's chances of acceptance.

The document finally agreed to at Weimar was a mix of elements taken from England, France, and the United States in a complicated legal construction and with an often unhappy confusion of powers. The first part, largely based on Preuss's design, outlined a *bürgerliche Rechtsstaat*, but the second, "Grundrechte und Grundpflichten der Deutschen," contained a catalogue of substantial political demands that reflected the very different political views represented at Weimar.

Einheit, Freiheit, Gleichheit were there, too, but these general concepts could not channel specific material demands or reconcile competing claims. The result was a combination of neutral governmental forms and political aims incompatible with each other; these were left to the republic's practice to resolve on the basis of the "negotiated truce between the classes" that had been achieved at Weimar.[45]

The crux of Weimar's later—and ultimate—dilemma lay in the ambiguity of the democratic principle and the frequently unworkable structure of its parliamentary government.[46] Although the democratic principle in article 1—the assertion that all legitimate power comes from the people—found wide acceptance in Germany after 1919 among political theorists and lawyers,[47] the debate on parliamentarism turned on the question of how this principle might be made workable in Weimar.

Although in terms of the alternatives available in 1918–1919, parliamentary democracy was in fact the conservative solution to Germany's constitutional problem, hostility toward the parties and parliamentary politics crippled it from the start. Even before the onset of serious parliamentary crisis, some were already complaining that the Weimar constitution had given Germany "nothing but a sorry party government."[48] Opposition to parliamentarism in Weimar came from three sources: traditional-authoritarian critics, who preferred the monarchical and bureaucratic system of the *Kaiserreich*; nationalists such as Hitler and the men around him, who hoped to combine social change with dictatorial government; and the radical left, for whom the Russian model and a dictatorship of the proletariat were the goal. In addition to these fundamentally opposed views of parliamentary democracy, there was a large body of critical academic literature in Europe and America on aspects of parliamentarism and on the causes of "continuing governmental crises" in many parliamentary states.[49]

European socialists first set out one of the most important theses in the contemporary literature on parliamentarism. They claimed that parliamentary politics was merely a shadow of political reality, an appearance created and manipulated by the network of overlapping interests in political parties, the press, and economic interest groups. In 1922, a year before *Die geistesgeschichtliche Lage des heutigen Parlamentarismus* first appeared, Joseph Schumpeter incorporated this argument into his assessment of the prospects for socialism in Germany.[50] He began with the relationship between parliamentarism and modern mass democracy, and asserted that the vastly enlarged franchise made parliament a different institution than that described by liberal theory. He concluded that parliamentary institutions were fundamentally meaningless; their importance came only from what went on outside them, not from the politics of parliamentary debate as such. According to Schumpeter, "classes today orient themselves with respect to politics according to the means of production."[51] Classes are represented in parliament by their parties, but the real conflict occurs elsewhere, in the economy and society. Parliamentary debate is therefore, not a form of free discussion or deliberation, but merely one front in the class struggle.

Max Weber had understood parties as necessary agents of political education and organization in modern society, and he recognized that increasing democratization (extension of voting rights and the political mobilization of people who had not before participated in politics) meant that political bureaucracy would also increase. While Weber was principally concerned about the effect this would have on the quality of political life and leadership, he thought that political parties, with their professional organizations to mobilize voters and win support, would also appeal to an essentially irrational element in the public; that was the source of his greatest fears about democratically elected officials. Schumpeter's analysis of Weimar parliamentarism stressed this aspect, but within a Marxist critique of parliamentary politics: Parties carry on the class struggle, and their techniques are determined by the mass audience they hope to win over. Their central concern is to organize this mass as voters, and the substantial effects of this could be seen, Schumpeter asserted, in the quality of electoral campaigns. Irrational factors had become more important than debate on issues, and this could also be observed in Reichstag speeches. These were no longer addressed, as liberal theory assumed, to the floor, but rather to a mass audience outside. Moreover, although parties organized the masses to vote, it was entirely unclear what exactly they were being organized for. Extending the franchise had not resulted in more democratic government, Schumpeter maintained; universal suffrage only transformed representation into a party system with new methods to capture voters, a new electoral machine, new party organizations and hierarchies. That alone, his argument continues,

disposes of rational argument because the size of the groups will burst those bounds within which it is effective; that creates the professional agitator, the party functionary, the Boss. That makes political success a question of organization and produces the various leadership circles and lobbies who make the MPs their puppets. That makes parliament itself a puppet, because agitation and victories outside it will be more important than a good speech in the house. Because now everyone is legally entitled to speak, no one will be able to speak except as the master of a machine. That has destroyed the original sense of parliament, broken its original technique, made its activity look like a farce.[52]

Parties dominated by elites increasingly represented particular social classes and corporative interests. Although these could work with each other and reach compromises, they had "basically nothing to deliberate or discuss with each other."[53] In contrast to parliamentary principles, the modern political machine was evolving into an executive that would act, not talk. This was Carl Schmitt's view too, and by 1923 he was certain that these structural changes had made discussion and openness, the principles of parliamentarism, a meaningless façade: "Small and exclusive committees of parties or of party coalitions make their decisions behind closed doors, and what representatives of the big capitalist interest groups agree to in the smallest committees is more important for the fate of millions of people, perhaps, than any political decision."[54]

Schmitt's view that parliament had become an "antechamber" for concealed interests and that its members were no longer, as the *Reichs-*

verfassung declared them, "representatives of the entire people
. . . bound only to their consciences and not to any instructions"
(article 21) was shared by Gustav Radbruch.[55] Writing in the first issue
of *Die Gesellschaft*, Radbruch offered a general critique of contemporary
German political culture as "driving politics to religion." He meant
that the political parties had developed as tightly bound, programmatic
interests incompatible with the principles of parliamentarism. Arguing
from a Social Democratic perspective, Radbruch rejected the con-
demnation by Marxists like Schumpeter of parliamentary politics as
a means to further working-class interests and urged responsible participation in coalition government: "Only in coalitions can the division
of power between capital and labor that dominates our society receive
a political expression. . . . One can also further the class struggle at
the negotiating table."[56] Still, Radbruch thought that parliament was
a showplace. "So long as it governs," he wrote in 1924, "then in
reality, not parliament, but the interests and voices of extraparliamentary circles that would like to gain influence on the parties, which
are extremely sensitive to pressure, rule."[57] More interesting than
Radbruch's polemics about the "grotesque show of every new governmental crisis" is his analysis of the relationship between a statesman
and a political program. The readiness to throw overboard every
program "when the idea of the state demands it" characterizes the
statesman and distinguishes him from the party politician, but the
statesman can only emerge when he enjoys the trust of his party.
The best relationships between party leaders and the parliamentary
party are built on trust, and so too is the relationship between the
voters and their representative: "The more politics ceases to be a
simple matter of fulfilling party demands, the more it takes place in
the area of finely colored compromises, just that much more impossible
it becomes to make these clear to the voters, who are naturally party-
voters in their great majority, if there is not a personal basis for trust
in their representatives in parliament."[58] Under German political conditions, Radbruch argued, the office of Reichspräsident took on a
special importance:

If democracy and parliamentarism are to function, a scale of trust and increasing independence of action must be constructed from the voters in the country through their representatives all the way to the leading statesmen. Among these the Reichspräsident has a special place. . . . The Reichspräsident is politically obliged to take appropriate measures if the government, which is responsible only to the parliamentary majority in the Reichstag, asks it of him . . . and to represent the republic with tact and dignity. . . . Against the purely ceremonial interpretation of this office, another fact must be taken into consideration: that the constitution has given the Reichspräsident a fundamentally different political foundation from that of the Reich government based on the parliament, the important foundation of direct election by the people.[59]

The debate on presidential power in early Weimar

The constitution gave the Reichspräsident a role in the dissolution of the Reichstag and the formation of a government; it also allowed him to appeal over the head of parliament to the German people directly. Of the powers assigned to the office of president in this system the most important were ultimately those in article 48. It authorized the Reichspräsident to use force against recalcitrant or rebellious Länder (*Reichsexecution*) or when "public security and order are seriously disturbed or endangered."

Between 1919 and 1924, and especially during the state crisis of 1923, these powers were used by Friedrich Ebert in a series of cases: against Thuringia and Gotha (1920); against Saxony (1923); and after Hitler's Beer Hall *Putsch* on November 8–9, 1923, executive authority in the Reich was delegated to the military under General von Seeckt. In addition to these cases of *Reichsexecution* against the Länder, Ebert also used the powers in section 2 of article 48 to put down political unrest and *Putsch* attempts (1920 and 1923) and disturbances following the assassinations of Erzberger (1921) and Rathenau (1922). From the end of 1922 numerous presidential orders aimed at the resolution of financial and economic problems were issued on the basis of powers in this article. In addition to decrees affecting currency and finance (to control foreign currency speculation and exchange and, after the stabilization of the mark, to initiate the transition to the new currency), a succession of taxation decrees was issued in winter 1923–1924.[60]

Only after the use of presidential powers subsided did constitutional lawyers and political theorists in Germany begin to debate the issue. Article 48 was discussed at the Jena conference of the Vereinigung der Deutschen Staatsrechtslehrer in April 1924 and at the Deutsche Juristentag the same year, and a series of articles appeared in the next five years on the legal and constitutional problems raised by the use of article 48 during the first years of unrest in the Republic.[61] This debate was largely dominated by the question of judicial review of the president's use of article 48 and by the question of "implicit legislative powers" the president might have under its authority— questions that followed directly from the political practice of the early 1920s.[62]

Carl Schmitt's paper at Jena, "Die Diktatur des Reichspräsident nach Artikel 48 der Reichsverfassung," took a different approach. Schmitt argued for interpretation of article 48 as providing a "commissarial dictatorship," a conception derived from *Die Diktatur* (1921), his study of the idea of dictatorship in modern political thought.[63] According to Schmitt, the president was empowered to act for "the security and defense of the constitution as a whole," which was "unimpeachable."[64] But Schmitt's interpretation of the president's wide-ranging commissarial powers met with little success, and the debate on article 48 continued during the middle years of the Republic (1924–1929) to focus on the legislative definition of executive authority under its provisions.[65] Schmitt, too, put the question aside until 1929. Only later, in the last crisis of the Republic, did the interpretation Schmitt (along with Erwin Jacobi) first suggested in 1924 take on practical political meaning and win support as a means to govern Germany without the check of parliament.[66] But the steps toward that view were long and indirect. Their path lay over the development of a constitutional interpretation and a theory of its protection that grew out of Schmitt's critique of parliamentarism and his preoccupation with the consequences of legal positivism.

Representative versus plebiscitary democracy

Richard Thoma's judgment in 1930 that "German democracy is overwhelmingly and fundamentally liberal and indirect, in contrast to an egalitarian-radical democratism [*sic*] to whose demands only very few concessions were given in the Weimar constitution,"[67] echoed his interpretation of the Republic's democratic principle in its first years. His article "Der Begriff der modernen Demokratie" (1922)[68] identified democracy with "formal democracy" or the extension of universal suffrage in a state; a democracy is, Thoma argued, the negation of an authoritarian state (*Obrigkeitsstaat*), "responsible government" as opposed to autocratic government. But the crucial aspect of Thoma's argument was his denial that democracy implied any substantial beliefs or politics; rather, in his view, democracy was a matter of forms and procedures, such as the secrecy of ballots, majority rule, and due process. In terms of this concept, Thoma argued, the German Republic was a liberal democracy: The parties were required for its functioning, and its workings as a democratic system depended on indirect expression of the popular will. Thoma contrasted Weimar's liberal, indirect democracy to radical democracy based on egalitarianism, plebiscitary elections, and referenda. Writing in the same year, Rudolf Smend also noted that parliamentary government was typical of the "*bürgerlich*-liberal culture of the nineteenth century, originally represented by the rationalistic belief in the productive power of a political dialectic as the form of the automatic achievement of political truth—in the classical age of English 'government by talking,' it was the form in which the political world of a country was represented with more or less absorption."[69] In such states, Smend concluded, the substantial, real contents of political life were secondary, except for the general attachment to liberty; the primary integration factors were elections, ministerial responsibility, budgetary decisions, and procedural regulation. But though Smend shared Thoma's concern for the formal properties of a democratic state, his discussion did not (like Thoma's) stop with these: "The precondition of the modern [state] is integration [and] the education of individuals through a value position . . . which must be constantly renewed by the functional-dialectical means of integration."[70] Just how the integrative means of parliamentarism do function will change through time. For Smend as for Schmitt, the underlying question of the democratic state in Germany was posed by the combination of parliamentary means and the realities of modern mass democracy. If parliamentarism could integrate the bourgeoisie in England during the nineteenth century, could it do the same for the newly political classes of Germany after the First World War?

The implicit answer of Carl Schmitt's *Parlamentarismus* was no. In the first edition of the essay Schmitt distinguished democracy from parliamentarism in terms a concept of "the people." Concretely the people are various and heterogeneous; but as the subject of democracy, the people are identical with the state: "The essence of the democratic principle . . . is the assertion that the law and the will of the people are identical."[71] Furthermore, the logic of democratic argument rests on a series of identities—the identity of rulers and ruled, governed and governing, subject and object of state authority, the people and their representatives in parliament, the state and the voters, the state and the law. Finally Schmitt argued that a democracy implied the identity of the quantitative (the numerical majority or plurality) with the qualitative (justice). Although Schmitt's conception of democratic homogeneity has frequently been misinterpreted as simply requiring that the people be a naturally (or racially) homogeneous community,[72] in fact the argument made in this first edition of *Parlamentarismus* does not depend on any such homogeneity. Rather, it was directed toward the theoretical question of political will in a democracy. This is clear from Schmitt's rather short discussion of electoral laws and the various means of expressing "the people's will" in a democracy. In later works this aspect of Schmitt's argument was developed as a theory of plebiscitary democracy.

The emergence of this conception of democracy in Schmitt's political thought during the early 1920s followed from his analysis of the democratic and liberal principles in the Weimar constitution. The Reich constitution and the constitutions of the German Länder, too, made provision for institutions of direct democracy. The Weimar constitution recognized five cases for the use of a plebiscite (*Volksentscheid*).[73] The Reichspräsident could ask for a plebiscite on a law concluded by the Reichstag (article 73), and the Reichsrat could ask the Reichspräsident to call for a plebiscite on the same grounds (article 74, section 3); the Reichsrat could ask for a plebiscite on a constitutional change initiated by the Reichstag (article 76, section 2); one-twentieth of the eligible voters could require a law that had been passed but set aside by the Reichstag to become the object of a plebiscite (article 73, section 2); and finally one-tenth of the electorate could petition for the introduction of a law on the basis of a referendum. If this law were enacted by the Reichstag, then "the referendum did not take place" (article 73, section 3). In a paper given on December 11, 1926, to the Berlin Juristische Gesellschaft,[74] Schmitt analyzed constitutional law in Weimar governing these provisions for direct democracy and tried to outline a theory of "the people" in democracy that was both modern and useful for jurisprudence.

Of those cases in which plebiscitary action can be taken, the constitution's provision for legislative initiative (article 73, sections 2 and 3) interested Schmitt most. He argued that "the people . . . under this section became active as the legislator,"[75] and that this section gave life to the democratic principle of the constitution as Schmitt understood it. The preamble to the Weimar constitution asserted that "the people have given themselves this constitution," and it had been Hugo Preuss's intention to develop a constitutional formula that incorporated the "constitutional power" of the German people.

Much of the tension in Schmitt's argument for plebiscitary democracy and the controversy it caused stemmed from a conception not fully worked out in his thought at this time. Schmitt aserted that the essence of the Weimar constitution was the democratic principle expressed in article 1, not its liberal principles (the provisions for parliamentary government and the legislative powers of the Reichstag). The special powers of the Reichspräsident were intended, so he argued, to secure this principle when it was threatened, allowing him to act as a "commissarial dictator" to preserve the structure of the Reich. Against the "oversimplified" division of representative versus direct democracy, Schmitt tried to show in 1926 that the Weimar constitution provided a more complicated democratic principle.

Schmitt did not at this time (or at any other during the republic) call for the suspension of elections; his argument was directed instead toward the moderation of parliamentary powers through other institutional means. But it should be clear from his argument in *Parlamentarismus* that Carl Schmitt had little respect for the procedures of liberal democracy as such. The secret ballot, individual voting rights—the whole structure of elections in a representative system seemed to him something politically quite distinct from democracy in modern states. Moreover, he believed that the intellectual and moral foundations of these institutions were already weakened by mass democracy and threatened by the appearance of Bolshevism and Fascism, more vital ideologies than liberalism. But his argument between 1923 and 1926 persuaded few opponents. Read together with his other contemporary works—*Politische Romantik* (1919), *Die Diktatur* (1921), *Politische Theologie* (1922), and *Römischer Katholizismus und politischer Form* (1923)—*Die geistesgeschichtliche Lage des heutigen Parlamentarismus* already seemed to those who stressed the indirect and liberal elements of the Weimar constitution, like Thoma, an attack on democracy as they understood it. Carl Schmitt's argument for the direct democratic elements of the constitution was certainly not meant to support democracy in the form Preuss and Weber had so opposed in 1918–1919; by 1926 the discussion in German state theory had in any case moved on. What, then, was the context in which Schmitt argued?

Legal positivism and legitimacy

The ultimate target of his political thought was the German theory
of legal positivism, whose roots lay in the mid nineteenth century.
The school founded by Carl Friedrich von Gerber and carried on by
Paul Laband at first provided a clear and modern alternative to the
historical school of law. But by the First World War the value-free
perspective of German legal positivism, which separated the law from
political and moral inquiry, was no longer capable of formulating
questions about the legitimacy of the state and political power or a
concept of justice that was relevant to the relationship of power and
authority in the state. These were dismissed as metaphysical and thus
unanswerable. Instead, German legal theorists developed a principle
of "the normative power of the factual," first stated by Georg Meyer.
Gerhard Anschütz accepted Meyer's view and provided the standard
formulation of it: "The capacity to use state power is not defined
through rightful inheritance [*rechtsmässigen Erwerb*] but through its actual
possession. . . . The question of the legitimacy of state power can
[certainly] be decided according to the principles of law; but the properties of state power as legitimate [can] exercise no particular legal
effect. Legitimacy is not a characteristic of state power."[76] After the
German revolution this legal theory was helpless even to define a
change as "revolutionary." "It demanded for its vitality," E. R. Huber
has written, "neither the 'permanent use' of the constitution produced
by the revolution, nor its sanction through 'a sense of justice' on the
part of those concerned. . . . [According to this theory] there was only
one ground of validity for a revolutionary constitution that arose from
the usurpation of state power: the actual possession of power."[77] Although Georg Jellinek's *Allgemeine Staatslehre* (1900)[78] modified this
view somewhat by introducing considerations of "convictions" (*Über-
zeugungen*), these were not conceived as truly normative. Rather they
were the product of an unchallenged use of power: "Customary right
does not come from the national spirit [*Volksgeist*] that sanctions it, [or]

from the convictions of the entire people that something might be right because of its inner necessity, [or] from the unspoken will of the people, but from general psychological qualities that see the consistently repeated fact as the norm."[79] In this way, German legal positivism divided questions about the relationship of power and justice: Its constitutional theory, like its jurisprudence, separated *Rechtsmässigkeit* from *Rechtswirksamkeit*, the justice of the laws from their effectiveness. It followed from this that the illegitimate conquest of state power was inconceivable; its actual occurrence in revolution could not affect the law's validity or a citizen's obligation.

Legal positivism was politically neutral. It could be used to justify an actually successful revolution just as much as a future, hypothetical revolution. Because of its theoretical ambivalence, legal positivism in Germany thus offered "no lasting guarantee for the validity of a constitution established through revolution."[80] The republican constitution might find "temporary legality" in *Rechtspositivismus*, but not "permanent legitimacy." Just how fragile this intellectual foundation was, very few German jurists recognized at the time. Most accepted Anschütz's interpretation of the constitution: "A revolution can be the new source of law if it successfully asserts its will and specifically if its law achieves recognition among those it governs."[81] Along with Rudolf Smend and Hermann Heller, Carl Schmitt rejected this view. It could not, he believed, offer clarity in jurisprudence, nor did it reveal the political sources of law and the state. By stressing the constitutional interpretation of the people's legislative power in the Republic and linking this to the office of the president, Schmitt thought that another basis for the Republic could be developed, one not dependent on the tenets of legal positivism.

Decision, discussion, and political values in Weimar

At this time in the Republic's history Schmitt was virtually alone among constitutional lawyers in his view of the institutions of parliament and plebiscitary democracy. Moritz Julius Bonn agreed with him that "there is a parliamentarism without democracy"[82] but resisted Schmitt's reduction of parliament to the principles of openness and discussion. He also objected to the concept of discussion advanced by Schmitt in *Parlamentarismus*. According to Bonn, "parliamentary discussion is not only discussion that wants to persuade the opponent of the falsehood of his views, but a discussion whose purpose is give-and-take, negotiation. . . . I am certain that there has always been a very close connection between ideologies and interests in parliamentarism, especially in tax matters. The two businessmen you talk about act in a thoroughly recognizable manner as parliamentarians in the most glorious age of the old parliamentarism."[83] Whereas Schmitt had asserted in *Politische Theologie* that "the opposite of discussion is dictatorship,"[84] Bonn wrote to him that "the proponents of dictatorship also want discussion, first of all because men are gregarious by nature." Further, the essence of parliamentary government was not "discussion" in Schmitt's sense, but something closer to "conference"; the opposite of this is "government by violence."[85]

Later in the 1920s, Hermann Heller's critique of Schmitt's *Begriff des Politischen* (1927), "Politische Demokratie und soziale Homogenität" (1928), while critical of Schmitt's principle of substantial social homogeneity in democracy, accepted the most important element in Schmitt's analysis.[86] Heller too emphasized the role of political values in democracy as living factors in its success, but he pushed Schmitt's argument further:

Actually the intellectual [*geistesgeschichtliche*] basis of parliamentarism is not the belief in public discussion as such, but belief in the existence of a common ground for discussion and in *fair play* for the opponent, with whom one wants to reach agreement under conditions that exclude naked force.[87]

Although Heller agreed that "a certain degree of social homogeneity is necessary for the construction of democratic unity," he insisted that "it can never mean the elimination of the necessarily antagonistic social structure."[88] Any attempt to remove these conflicts on the basis

Ellen Kennedy

of a unitary moral principle must lead, Heller thought, to repression and injustice. At the beginning of the Great Depression, Heller's "Rechtsstaat oder Diktatur?" posed the question of social justice and constitutional stability in the starkest terms: Either the parliamentary principle would be expanded from political to social and economic issues and there produce the predictability on which the idea of the *Rechtsstaat* is founded as a *soziale Rechtsstaat*," or Germany would succumb to dictatorship. There were no other alternatives.[89]

In the last year of the Republic, Schmitt and Heller found themselves on opposing sides in the one great court case of the Republic that reviewed the powers of the president and the Reichstag under article 48.[90] By then German parliamentary democracy was already in eclipse, and the next year Hitler's appointment by Hindenburg wiped away the remnants of German democracy not only as Thoma, Smend, Bonn, and Heller understood it but also in Carl Schmitt's view. In late Weimar, Schmitt's theory was fully developed in a critique of empiricism in political science and an assertion that the spirit of the Weimar constitution could be protected at the expense of its letter. By then Schmitt regarded the Reichstag as the most dangerous element in Weimar; only the Reichspräsident offered any hope for the defeat of "unconstitutional" parties. Years later Schmitt saw his work during 1929–1932 as "a warning and a cry for help" for effective action to stop the Nazis. That it failed is a matter of history. Had it succeeded, the changes Schmitt advocated might have included, as one commentator suggested, developing the constitution along the lines of its inner consistencies.[91] But the thread of these had led Carl Schmitt away from even the modest hope he had for parliamentary government in the early 1920s.

Conclusion

Constitutional law and politics in the Weimar Republic were the immediate occasion for Carl Schmitt's *Parlamentarismus* and it belongs to a debate on the fundamental institutions of liberal democracy in the first German republic. Schmitt's text was not an isolated example of the concern many Germans felt at the instability of parliamentary government and the uncertain authority of Weimar's political institutions. But Schmitt's analysis of these problems is distinguished from most contemporary comment by the emphasis he placed on "the intellectual foundations of a specifically intended institution." He aimed at an explanation of "the ultimate core of the institution of modern parliament" and believed he had found it in discussion and openness.[92] Only on the basis of this knowledge could the crisis of parliamentarism be understood and reform of parliamentary democracy undertaken. Richard Thoma thought this the book's weakness, Rudolf Smend saw it as Schmitt's strength. Hermann Heller agreed that part of the crisis of parliamentarism in Weimar was normative, but he disagreed with Schmitt on its cause and cure. Yet all his readers and contemporaries agreed on one point: the radicalism of Schmitt's approach, not just to the idea and institution of parliament, but to the assumptions of liberal political thought as a whole.

Schmitt's political science broke apart the conception of liberal democracy by starting with an apparently unpolitical theme, truth and reason. Following this thread through the history of liberalism led Schmitt, as Rudolf Smend recognized, to see the "dynamic-dialectic" of parliamentarism first in parliamentary institutions as the political agent of enlightened opinion and, second, in the structure of public opinion that should check and inform political decision. In the first, liberal theory sets a practical precondition for the attainment of truth (and hence justice) in political life in the idea of a free mandate for the people's representatives in parliament. If practice contradicts this idea—if representatives speak and act on behalf of particular interests or as delegates of their parties—the legitimacy of parliamentarism undergoes a fundamental change. The issue of parliamentary integrity and the notion of free and open discussion that is bound up with it is a question not simply of the incorruptibility of legislators (although this is one important aspect of it) but also of the process of legislation itself.

Contemporary political theory in Germany has built on this aspect of Schmitt's argument in *Parlamentarismus* while maintaining a critical distance from his political thought as a whole. Although skeptical of neoconservatives' use of Schmitt, Jürgen Habermas's *Strukturwandel der Öffentlichkeit* (1962) begins with a question about the paradoxical development of *Öffentlichkeit* that assumes much of Schmitt's argument. While the public sphere [*Öffentlichkeit*] has steadily widened, Habermas notes, its function has become weaker. Despite this transformation in practice, *Öffentlichkeit* still remains an organizational principle and norm in liberal political systems.[93] The political dimension of this transformation in the structure of the public sphere lies for Habermas and for Otto Kirchheimer in the disintegration of the coherence of "the public." The dissolution of the public does not remain isolated in the theory of political culture, but, according to Habermas and Kirchheimer, calls into question the central institutions of liberal democracy.[94]

Carl Schmitt had already linked this transformation in political culture and institutions to technological changes in the media of *Öffentlichkeit* and in their political economy. The literate culture that fostered classical liberalism and was in turn sheltered by its political successes placed a special emphasis on the press as the principal instrumentality of an enlightened public and good government. Just after the First World War, Ferdinand Tönnies's *Kritik der öffentliche Meinung* (1922) demonstrated that liberal theory misstated the social function of the press in relation to public opinion; the press was far more active in the creation of opinion than early liberal theorists imagined. In the decade after this study appeared, sociologists extended Tönnies's inquiry into a general question about the role of the press and public opinion in the modern state.

In the course of this debate Carl Schmitt pointed to a basic difference between the press's traditional function and status within liberal theory and the new public media of radio. At the 1930 conference of German sociologists in Berlin, Carl Brinkmann argued that development of the press as an agent in the creation of public opinion made its neutralization essential. That, so Brinkmann maintained, would restore the position of the free press within liberalism and eliminate the distortions of political interest. In reply, Schmitt pointed out that such neutralization was both politically naive and practically impossible. Radio in this scheme of things would either become amusement and thus "indifferent" or, through the notion of a parity of access, all political parties would be given an "equal chance" in its use. Either way radio must be seen as a qualitatively different medium: "There are enormous powers at work here, and we do not know what they are and whether they will increase."[95]

Much of what Carl Schmitt later proposed as a solution to the problems inherent in the "dynamic-dialectic" of discussion and openness now seems, when viewed through the experience of Weimar and Euopean dictatorship between the wars, dangerous and destructive. In Germany, where his influence has been most profound, Schmitt's political theory remains burdened by a tendency to blame the bearer for the bad news; elsewhere, now as then, "there are certainly not very many people who want to renounce the old liberal freedoms,"[96] but even fewer who have grasped with such clarity as Carl Schmitt the intellectual foundations of these freedoms and their democratic complications. The problem remains the same, and it makes the central dilemma of the Weimar Republic—the balance and interaction of liberal institutions and the democratic principle—our own.

Notes

1. The quotations in this paragraph are taken from Robert Leicht, "Ein Staatsrecht ohne das Recht: Über die Machtphantasien eines Unpolitischen," *Süddeutsche Zeitung*, No. 154, July 8-9, 1978, and Christian Graf von Krockow, "Freund oder Feind: Parlamentarismus oder Diktatur—Die Unheimliche Aktualität und Kontinuität des Carl Schmitt," *Die Zeit*, No. 46, November 11, 1983. See also Ellen Kennedy, "Carl Schmitt in West German Perspective," *West European Politics* 4 (1984), 120-127.

Ellen Kennedy

2. Richard Thoma, "Zur Ideologie des Parlamentarismus und der Diktatur," *Archiv für Sozialwissenschaft und Sozialpolitik* 53 (1925), 215–217.

3. Carl Schmitt, *Römischer Katholizismus und politische Form* (Hellerau: Jakob Hegner Verlag, 1923). The second edition was published with the Imprimatur (Munich & Rome: Theatiner Verlag, 1925). An English translation by E. M. Codd with an introduction by Christopher Dawson appeared in the series "Essays in Order" as *The Necessity of Politics: An Essay on the Representative Idea in the Church and Modern Europe* (London: Sheed & Ward, 1931).

4. Muth to Schmitt, June 6, 1926. Among Schmitt's closest circle of admirers at this time were Hugo Ball and Waldimar Gurian; Ball wrote that "as a Catholic thinker Schmitt is a new type of Kant," and when reviewing Schmitt's *Politische Theologie* (1922) for *Hochland*, Ball praised Schmitt's defense of Catholicism and European civilization. During these years Schmitt published frequently in leading Catholic journals; in addition to Hochland, he wrote for the *Kölnische Volkszeitung* and for *Germania*, the journal of the Catholic Zentrum (Center party). An account of Schmitt's political associations during these years can be found in Joseph W. Bendersky, *Carl Schmitt: Theorist for the Reich* (Princeton: Princeton University Press, 1983).

5. *Bonner Festgabe für Ernst Zitelmann* (Munich & Leipzig: Duncker & Humblot, 1923). Schmitt's *Parlamentarismus* was also published by Duncker & Humblot in 1923 as a separate brochure.

6. Schmitt to Muth, March 10, 1926.

7. Feuchtwanger to Schmitt, May 14, 1926.

8. Feuchtwanger to Schmitt, December 5, 1925. Schmitt's *Parlamentarismus* appeared as volume one in the series "Wissenschaftliche Abhandlungen und Reden zur Philosophie, Politik und Geistesgeschichte" simultaneously with the following: Max Weber, *Politik als Beruf* (vol. 2); Erich Becher, *Metaphysik und Naturwissenschaften* (vol. 3); and Georg Simmel, *Der Konflikt der modernen Kultur* (vol. 4). All subsequent editions were issued as part of the series, until the fourth edition (1961) appeared when the essay was published independently.

9. Schmitt to Feuchtwanger, December 8, 1925.

10. Feuchtwanger to Schmitt, May 14, 1926.

11. Carl Schmitt, *Politische Romantik* (Munich & Leipzig: Duncker & Humblot, 1919).

12. Carl Schmitt, *Die Diktatur. Von den Anfängen des modernen Souveränitätsgedankens bis zum proletarischen Klassenkampf* (Munich & Leipzig: Duncker & Humblot, 1921). See also the earlier articles "Diktatur und Belagerungszustand," *Zeitschrift für die gesamte Strafrechtswissenschaft* 38 (1916), 138–162, and "Die Einwirkung des Kriegszustands auf das ordentliche strafprozessuale Verfahren," *Zeitschrift für die gesamte Strafrechtswissenschaft* 38 (1916), 783–793.

13. Carl Schmitt, *Politische Theologie. Vier Kapital zur Lehre von der Souveränität* (Munich & Leipzig: Duncker & Humblot, 1922).

14. Ibid., 78.

15. Carl Schmitt, "Der Gegensatz von Parlamentarismus und moderner Massendemokratie," *Hochland* 23 (1926), 257–270.

16. Carl Schmitt, *Volksentscheid und Volksbegehren. Ein Beitrag zur Auslegung der Weimarer Verfassung und zur Lehre von der unmittelbaren Demokratie* (Berlin & Leipzig: Walter de Grutyer & Co., 1927). This text is an expanded version of a lecture given on December 11, 1926.

17. Rudolf Smend, *Verfassung und Verfassungsrecht* (1928), in Smend, *Staatsrechtliche Abhandlungen und andere Aufsätze*, 2d ed. (Berlin: Duncker & Humblot, 1968), 152 (1st ed., 1955).

18. Thoma, "Zur Ideologie des Parlamentarismus." Compared to Weber and Preuss, Friedrich Naumann exercised little influence on Carl Schmitt; it could also be argued that despite Thoma's view of them as roughly equal in their influence, Naumann's ideas played a much smaller part in the shape of the Weimar constitution than did the thought of the others. But see Theodor Heuss, *Friedrich Naumann: Der Mann, Das Werk* (Stuttgart: Deutsche Verlags-Anstalt, 1949), and Naumann's *Werke*, ed. Theodor Schieder, Wolfgang Mommsen, el al. (Cologne & Opladen: Westdeutscher Verlag, 1964).

19. See this volume, 20.

20. See this volume, 49.

21. Ibid.

22. Harold Laski, *The Foundations of Sovereignty* (New York: Harcourt Brace & Co., 1921). Lord Acton complained that the Swiss constitution of 1874 was "separating decision from deliberation" because it provided for plebiscites. See Acton's review of Erskine May's *Democracy in Europe* (1877) in Acton's *The History of Freedom and Other Essays* (London: Macmillan, 1907). It is not clear from Laski's text whether he knew Acton's essay or not, but Carl Schmitt certainly takes the phrase from Laski, not Acton.

23. See this volume, 35.

24. See for example Leo Wittmayer's review of the first edition of *Parlamentarismus* in the *Archiv des öffentlichen Rechts* 47/N.F.8 (1925), 231–233. Wittmayer was the author of *Deutscher Reichstag und Reichsregierung* (1918), *Die Weimarer Reichsverfassung* (1922), and *Parlamentarismus und Demokratie* (1928).

25. George Schwab, *The Challenge of the Exception: An Introduction to the Political Ideas of Carl Schmitt between 1921 and 1936* (Berlin: Duncker & Humblot, 1970), 61.

Ellen Kennedy

26. Article 1 of the Weimar constitution reads: "The German Reich is a republic. State power comes from the people." Horst Hildebrandt, ed., *Die deutschen Verfassungen des 19. und 20. Jahrhunderts* (Paderborn: Schöningh, 1979), 69.

Willibalt Apelt writes that the calling of the National Assembly meant that in "Germany too Rousseau's political theory that sovereignty, including the determination of the law, the form of the state, and its constitution, rests with the people had now been accepted." Apelt too identifies parliamentarism with democracy, in this case because the alternatives—monarchy or the dictatorship of the proletariat—represented the dominance of one man or one class. Apelt, *Die Geschichte der Weimarer Verfassung* (Munich & Berlin: Beck'sche Verlagsbuchhandlung, 1965), 47–48.

27. Richard Thoma, "Das Reich als Demokratie," in Gerhard Anschütz and Richard Thoma, eds., *Handbuch des Deutschen Staatsrechts* (Tübingen: Mohr, 1929).

28. Karl Dietrich Bracher, *Die Auflösung der Weimarer Republik. Eine Studie zum Problem des Machtverfalls in der Demokratie* (Königstein/Ts.: Droste Verlag, 1978), 19.

29. Hugo Preuss, "Volksstaat oder Verkehrter Obrigkeitsstaat?", *Berliner Tageblatt*, Nr. 583, November 11, 1918, in Preuss, *Staat, Recht und Freiheit. Aus 40 Jahren Deutsche Politik* (Tübingen: Mohr, 1926), 366. On Hugo Preuss's place in the history of the Weimar constitution, see Apelt, *Die Geschichte der Weimarer Verfassung*, 55ff., and the introduction by Theodor Heuss to *Staat, Recht und Freiheit*. Carl Schmitt regarded Preuss's essay "Volksstaat oder Verkehrter Obrigkeitsstaat?" as "one of the most important documents of German constitutional history." Schmitt, *Hugo Preuss: Sein Staatsbegriff und seine Stellung in der Deutschen Staatslehre* (Tübingen: Mohr, 1930), 17. A similar position is taken by Apelt, who, like Schmitt, sees Preuss as the single most important intellectual force in defeating Bolshevism and reaction in 1918–1919; see Schmitt, *Hugo Preuss*, 56ff. Preuss's "Volksstaat oder Verkehrter Obrigkeitsstaat?" appeared on the morning of his appointment by Ebert as Staatssekretär in the Interior Ministry.

30. Preuss, *Staat, Recht und Freiheit*, 365.

31. Ibid., 367.

32. Ibid., 366.

33. Hugo Preuss, "Denkschrift zum Entwurf des allgemeines Teils der Reichsverfassung vom 3. Januar 1919," *Reichsanzeiger*, January 20, 1919, in Preuss, *Staat, Recht und Freiheit*, 368–394.

34. Preuss, *Staat, Recht und Freiheit*, 370. Cf. Anschütz's characterization of Preuss's "dominant political principle" as "democratic unity," in *Verfassung des Deutschen Reichs vom 11. August 1919* (Berlin: G. Stilke, 1929), 17. See also Anschütz's discussion of parliament as the representative of the German people as a national whole (159ff.).

35. Max Weber, "Das neue Deutschland" (1918), in Johannes Winckelmann, ed., *Max Weber. Gesammelte Politische Schriften* (Tübingen: Mohr, 1980), 486.

Introduction

36. Max Weber, "Parlament und Regierung im neugeordneten Deutschland. Zur politische Kritik des Beamtentums und Parteiwesens" (1918), in Winckelmann, ed., *Max Weber*, 393. Walter Struve reduces Max Weber's concerns to a flat preference for elitism as a "device to promote the development of a state that would pursue a consistent policy of imperialism tapping fully the resources of the entire nation." Struve, *Elites against Democracy: Leadership Ideals in Bourgeois Political Thought in Germany, 1890–1933* (Princeton: Princeton University Press, 1973), 114. This really misses the point. For a very different, more sympathetic interpretation of Weber, see Wilhelm Hennis, "Max Weber's Central Question," *Economy and Society* 12 (1983), 135–180.

37. Winckelmann, ed., *Max Weber*, 394.

38. Ibid.

39. Max Weber, "Deutschlands künftige Staatsform" (1918), in Winckelmann, ed., *Max Weber*, 468ff.

40. Max Weber, "Der Reichspräsident" (1919), in Winckelmann, ed., *Max Weber*, 498.

41. Ibid., 500.

42. Robert Redslob, *Die parlamentarische Regierung in ihrer echten und in ihren unechten Form. Eine vergleichende Studie über die Verfassungen von England, Belgien, Ungarn, Schweden und Frankreich* (Tübingen: Mohr, 1918); Robert Piloty, *Das parlamentarische System. Eine Untersuchung seines Wesens und seines Wertes* (Berlin & Leipzig: Verlagsbuchhandlung Rothschild, 1917); Wilhelm Hasbach, *Die parlamentarische Kabinettsregierung ausserhalb England* (Leipzig: Deichert, 1918). See also Theodor Eschenberg, *Die improvisierte Demokratie. Gesammelte Aufsätze zur Weimarer Republik* (Munich: Piper & Co. Verlag, 1963), 41ff. An early but still telling critique of the conception held by this generation of German political scientists of parliamentarism and parliamentary government is Ulrich Scheuner, "Über die verschiedenen Gestaltungen des parlamentarischen Regierungssystems—zugleich eine Kritik der Lehre vom echten Parlamentarismus," *Archiv des öffentlichen Rechts* 13 (1927), 209-233, 337-380.

43. Weber, "Parlament und Regierung im neugeordneten Deutschland," in Winckelmann, ed., *Max Weber*, 383.

44. Thomas Mann, *Betrachtungen eines Unpolitischen* (1914 & 1919), quoted in Eschenberg, *Die improvisierte Demokratie*, 43.

45. In the committee of the National Assembly that dealt with the question of *Grundrechte* in the new constitution, Friedrich Naumann was confronted by two alternatives in the conception of a constitution: Either it was an expression of a unitary *Weltanschauung* and social structure, or it was the conclusion of a compromise between various social groups. Naumann opted for the latter and urged the National Assemby to accept "a negotiated truce between capitalism and socialism." See Naumann's "Bericht und Protokolle des 8 Ausschusses über den Entwurf einer Verfassung des Deutschen Reiches," *Berichte der Nationalversammlung* 21 (Berlin, 1920), 180. Quoted in Ingebourg Maus, *Bür-

gerliche Rechtstheorie und Faschismus. Zur sozialen Funktion und aktuellen Wirkung der Theorie Carl Schmitts (Munich: Fink Verlag, 1980), 27.

46. On Weimar's final crisis, see Bracher, *Die Auflösung*, and his article "Demokratie und Machtvakuum: Zum Problem des Parteienstaats in der Auflösung der Weimar Republik," in Karl Dietrich Erdmann and Hagen Schulze, eds., *Weimar: Selbstpreisgabe einer Demokratie. Eine Bilanz Heute* (Dusseldorf: Droste, 1980). See also Larry Eugene Jones, "The Dissolution of the Bourgeois Party System in the Weimar Republic," in Richard Bessel and E. J. Feuchtwanger, eds., *Social Change and Political Development in Weimar Germany* (London: Croom Helm, 1981).

47. In 1921 Hans Kelsen wrote that democracy was "nearly taken for granted in political thought," and for the Austro-Marxist Rudolf Hiferding it was "the only state form" possible after the mass experience of the 1914-1918 war. Richard Thoma, writing in 1923, divided all states into two simple categories: democracies and "privilege states." Schmitt makes the same point here, and by the late 1920s his standard work on the liberal *Rechtsstaat, Verfassungslehre* (1928), noted that "the legitimacy of the Weimar constitution rests on the constitutional power of the German people." Carl Schmitt, *Verfassungslehre* (Munich & Leipzig: Duncker & Humblot, 1928), 88.

48. Walter Schotte, "Der missverstandene Parlamentarismus," *Preussische Jahrbücher* 181 (1920), 134.

49. See this volume, 19.

50. Joseph Schumpeter, "Sozialistische Möglichkeiten von Heute," *Archiv für Sozialwissenschaft und Sozialpolitik* 48 (1922), 305-360; see also Carl Landauer's reply, "Sozialismus und parlamentarisches System," *Archiv für Sozialwissenschaft und Sozialpolitik* 48 (1922), 748-760. Schumpeter's view was not an isolated one on the left at this time. Max Adler wrote that parliamentary democracy is "a part of the class struggle: It's always the wielding of power [*Machtdurchsetzung*] by one class against another that with its majority wants to force its laws onto the resisting class." Max Adler, *Die Staatsauffassung des Marxismus. Ein Beitrag zur Unterscheidung von Soziologischer und Juristischer Methode* (Vienna: Wiener Volksbuchhandlung, 1922), 125. Adler's *Die Staatsauffassung des Marxismus* was an answer to Hans Kelsen's *Sozialismus und Staat* (1921). Adler's antiparliamentary views at this time are misrepresented in Tom Bottomore's introduction to *Austro-Marxism* (Oxford: Clarendon Press, 1978), which tends to stress the mixture of "revolutionary and reformist" elements within the school as a whole and pass over the much more enthusiastic view Adler in particular held of the Soviet Union at this time.

51. Schumpeter, "Sozialistische Möglichkeiten," 326.

52. Ibid., 329-330.

53. Ibid.

54. This volume, 49-50.

55. Gustav Radbruch, "Goldbilanz der Reichsverfassung," *Die Gesellschaft* 1 (1924), 57–69.

56. Ibid., 62. Compare Landauer, "Sozialismus und parlamentarisches System."

57. Radbruch, "Goldbilanz," 65.

58. Ibid., 65.

59. Ibid., 65–66. Radbruch was not alone in thinking that the office of Reichspräsident has a special place in the constitution; see also Hugo Preuss, "Reichsverfassungsmässige Diktatur," *Zeitschrift für Politik* 13 (1924), 97–113. Hermann Pünder comments that "Ebert in no sense shared the view that the office of the Reichspräsident was a decoration." Pünder, *Der Reichspräsident in der Weimarer Republik* (Bonn & Frankfurt/M: Athenäum Verlag, 1961), 17.

60. Ulrich Scheuner, "Die Anwendung des Art. 48 der Weimarer Reichsverfassung under den Präsidenten von Ebert und Hindenburg," in Ferdinand A. Hermens and Theodor Schieder, eds., *Staat, Wirtschaft und Politik in der Weimarer Republik* (Berlin: Duncker & Humblot, 1967), 249–286.

61. Ibid. "Die Diktatur des Reichspräsident," in *Veröffentlichungen der Vereinigungen der Deutschen Staatsrechtslehrer*, Heft 1 (Berlin: W. de Gruyter & Co., 1924), 63ff.

62. See Scheuner, "Art. 48," 266ff.

63. According to Schmitt, a "commissarial dictator" exercised power temporarily and for the purpose of restoring the already established constitutional order; a "sovereign dictator" creates a new constitutional order. See also Schwab, *The Challenge of the Exception*, 30–37.

64. Schmitt, *Die Diktatur*, ix.

65. Schmitt's paper at the 1924 conference of German constitutional lawyers (see note 61 above) was appended to the second edition of *Die Diktatur* (1927), 213–259. Hugo Preuss's view of Schmitt's interpretation of presidential powers in article 48 was an exception among German jurists. Commenting on Schmitt's view in a 1924 article, Preuss wrote: "This definition of the concept of dictatorship completely conforms to the essence of extraordinary power that is set out in article 48 of the Weimar constitution and given to the Reichspräsident." Preuss, "Reichsverfassungsmässige Diktatur," 101. See also Richard Grau, *Die Diktaturgewalt des Reichspräsident und der Landesregierungen auf Grund des Artikel 48 der Reichsverfassung* (Berlin: Liebmann, 1922). Grau argued that "the *Rechtsstaat* cannot preserve itself when threatened from within only by the means given in the division of powers." Grau further noted that these extraordinary powers "were firmly anchored in constitutional-legal responsibility." Grau, *Diktaturgewalt*, 104–105.

66. See Bendersky, *Carl Schmitt*, 145ff., and Ellen Kennedy, "Review Article, Joseph W. Bendersky, *Carl Schmitt: Theorist for the Reich*," *History of Political Thought* 4 (1983) 579–589.

67. Richard Thoma, "Sinn und Gestaltung des deutschen Parlamentarismus," in Bernard Harms, ed., *Recht und Staat im neuen Deutschland. Vorlesungen gehalten in der Deutschen Vereinigung für Staatswissenschaftliche Fortbildung*, vol. 1 (Berlin: Verlag von Reimar Hobbing, 1929), 114.

68. Richard Thoma, "Der Begriff der modernen Demokratie im seinem Verhältnis zum Staatsbegriff," in Melchior Palyi, ed., *Hauptprobleme der Soziologie. Erinnerungsgabe für Max Weber*, vol. 2 (Munich & Leipzig: Duncker & Humblot, 1922), 37–65.

69. Rudolf Smend, "Die politische Gewalt im Verfassungsstaat und das Problem der Staatsform" (1923), in Smend, *Staatsrechtliche Abhandlungen*, 85.

70. Ibid., 87.

71. This volume, 26.

72. For example, Charles E. Frye, "Carl Schmitt's Concept of the Political," *Journal of Politics* 28 (1966), 818–830.

73. Schmitt, *Volksentscheid und Volksbegehren*, 8. On the elements of direct democracy in Weimar, see Reinhard Schiffers, *Elemente direkter Demokratie im Weimarer Regierungssystem* (Dusseldorf: Droste, 1971), esp. 272ff.

74. Schmitt, *Volksentscheid und Volksbegehren*, 34.

75. Ibid., 9.

76. Gerhard Anschütz revised Meyer's *Lehrbuch des deutschen Staatsrechts* (1878), and later editions were published under both names: Georg Meyer and Gerhard Anschütz, *Lehrbuch des deutschen Staatsrechts* (Munich & Leipzig: Duncker & Humblot, 1906). Anschütz's formulation is quoted in E. R. Huber, *Deutsche Verfassungsgeschichte seit 1789*, vol. 6 (Stuttgart: Verlag W. Kohlhammer, 1981), 8. On legal positivism in Germany see also Peter Oertzen, *Die soziale Funktion des staatsrechtlichen Positivismus. Eine Studie über die Entstehung des formalistischen Positivismus in der deutschen Staatsrechtswissenschaft* (Frankfurt: Suhrkamp Verlag, 1974).

77. Huber, *Deutsche Verfassungsgeschichte*, vol. 6, 8.

78. Georg Jellinek, *Allgemeine Staatslehre* (Kronberg/Ts: Verlag Athenäum, 1977); the edition currently available is a reprint of the third (1921). *Allgemeine Staatslehre* first appeared in 1900. On representation and representative institutions, see pages 566ff.

79. Meyer and Anschütz, *Lehrbuch* (1914, 7th edition), 26, quoted in Huber, *Deutsche Verfassungsgeschichte*, vol. 6, 8.

80. Huber, *Deutsche Verfassungsgeschichte*, vol. 6, 9.

81. Ibid., 10.

82. Moritz Julius Bonn, *Die Auflösung des modernen Staates* (Berlin: Verlag für Politik und Wirtschaft, 1921), 24.

83. Bonn to Schmitt, June 11, 1926.

84. Schmitt, *Politische Theologie*, 78.

85. Bonn to Schmitt, June 11, 1926.

86. Carl Schmitt, "Der Begriff des Politischen," *Archiv für Sozialwissenschaft und Sozialpolitik* 58 (1927), 1-33. This article was originally a lecture in the Deutsche Hochschule für Politik, Berlin (May 1927). It was published in book form in 1932, along with another lecture entitled "Das Zeitalter der Neutralisierungen und Entpolitisierungen" (Tagung des Europäischen Kulturbundes, Barcelona, October 1929) and three corollaries. Schmitt, *Der Begriff des Politischen* (Munich & Leipzig: Duncker & Humblot, 1932). The English translation is by George Schwab, *The Concept of the Political* (New Brunswick, N.J.: Rutgers University Press, 1976).

87. Hermann Heller, "Politische Demokratie und soziale Homogenität" (1928), in Heller, *Gesammelte Schriften*, Ed. Christoph Müller, vol. 2 (Leiden: Sijthoff, 1971), 427. See also Ellen Kennedy, "The Politics of Toleration in Late Weimar: Hermann Heller's Analysis of Fascism and Political Culture," *History of Political Thought* 5 (1984), 109-127.

88. Heller, "Politische Demokratie," 427-428.

89. Hermann Heller, "Rechtsstaat oder Diktatur?" (1929), in Heller, *Gesammelte Schriften*, 443-462. See also Christoph Müller and Ilse Staff, eds., *Der soziale Rechtsstaat. Gedachtnisschrift für Hermann Heller* (Baden-Baden: Nomos Verlag, 1984), and Wolfgang Schluchter, *Entscheidung für den sozialen Rechtsstaat. Hermann Heller und die staatstheoretische Diskussion in der Weimarer Republik* (Baden-Baden: Nomos Verlag, 1983).

90. *Preussen contra Reich vor dem Staatsgerichtshof: Stenogrammbericht der Verhandlungen vor dem Staatsgerichtshof in Leipzig vom 10. bis 14. und vom 17. Oktober 1932* (Berlin: J. H. W. Dietz Nachf, 1933). See also Bendersky, *Carl Schmitt*, 154ff. and Kennedy "Review Article, Joseph W. Bendersky, *Carl Schmitt: Theorist for the Reich*."

91. Schwab, *The Challenge of the Exception*. Schmitt argued against the appointment of Hitler by Hindenburg. In the late 1950s, he saw his work in the last years of the republic, especially *Legalität und Legitimität* (Munich & Leipzig: Duncker & Humblot, 1932), as "a warning and a cry for help." Schmitt, *Verfassungsrechtliche Aufsätze aus den Jahren 1924–1954* (Berlin: Duncker & Humblot, 1958), 345ff. In Schmitt's view the leader of the Zentrum, Prälat Ludwig Kass, had a decisive influence on Hindenburg's appointment of Hitler as Reichskanzler; Kass attacked Schmitt's position as "illegal" in a letter on January 26, 1933, to then-chancellor Kurt von Schleicher. "Hitler used legality as his most powerful weapon" in the weeks before January 30, Schmitt wrote; "his [Hitler's] best instrument to influence Hindenburg was the threat of a new process before the Staatsgreichtshof. . . . For a man like Hindenburg, the thought of being drawn again into the outcry and chicanery of a tactical and propagandistic trial was unbearable"

Ellen Kennedy

(Ibid., 450). On this whole question, see Bendersky, *Carl Schmitt*, 185ff., especially the account of Schmitt's reply to Kass on p. 187. Excerpts from Schmitt's diaries published by Eberhard Straub indicate how depressed Schmitt was by the prospect of Hitler's appointment: "The Old Man [Hindenburg] has gone crazy" (January 27, 1933); "Cancelled my lecture. Couldn't work. Ridiculous state of affairs. Read the newspaper. Excited myself into a temper—so the day went" (January 31, 1933). See "Der Jurist im Zweilicht des Politischen: Carl Schmitt und der Staat," *Frankfurter Allgemeine Zeitung*, July 18, 1981.

92. Quotations in this sentence are from Schmitt, *Parlamentarismus*. See this volume, 20, 50.

93. Jürgen Habermas, *Strukturwandel del Öffentlichkeit. Untersuchungen zu einer Kategorie der bürgerlichen Gesellschaft* (Darmstadt & Neuwied: Luchterhand, 1962), 17. Habermas's very complicated intellectual relationship to Carl Schmitt cannot be treated in a footnote; but see for example Habermas's introduction to *Observations on "The Spiritual Situation of the Age"* (Cambridge, Mass.: MIT Press, 1984), esp. 12ff.

94. Habermas, "Das umfunktionierte Prinzip der Publizität," in *Strukturwandel*, esp. 343ff.; and Kirchheimer, "Majoritäten und Minoritäten in westeuropäischen Regierungen," *Die Neue Gesellschaft* 6 (1959), 256–270. For Kirchheimer's equally ambivalent relationship to Schmitt, see the collection *Von der Weimarer Republik zum Faschismus: Die Auflösung der demokratische Rechtsordung* (Frankfurt: Suhrkamp, 1976).

95. Carl Schmitt, "Diskussion über Presse und öffentliche Meinung," in *Verhandlungen der 7. Deutschen Soziologentages* (Tübingen: Mohr, 1931), 56–59. These are the proceedings of the conference of sociologists held in Berlin from September 28 to October 1, 1930. Schmitt's argument takes up Tönnies, *Kritik der öffentliche Meinung* (Berlin: Springer, 1922), esp. the discussion in chap. 3. Cf. Tönnies's long and critical review of Schmitt's *Parlamentarismus*, "Demokratie und Parlamentarismus," *Schmoller's Jahrbuch* 51 (1927), 1–44. Schmitt's remarks here should be read along with his argument in *Legalität und Legitimität* against an "equal chance" for anticonstitutional parties. There and here he mentions the Communist party (KPD) and the Nazis (NSDAP) and it is clear that they were his target. Neutrality in the face of these, he answered Carl Brinkmann in 1930, was just "a way of getting out of the struggle." Cf. Brinkmann, "Presse und öffentliche Meinung," *Verhandlungen der 7. Deutschen Soziologentages*, 9–31.

96. This volume, 50.

The Crisis of Parliamentary Democracy

Preface to the Second Edition (1926): On the Contradiction between Parliamentarism and Democracy

The second edition of this examination of the intellectual circumstances of contemporary parliamentarism remains essentially unchanged. This should not create the impression that I wish to lift it above any discussion. There are rather grounds for a somewhat contrary fear. A calm and factual debate that distances itself from all party-political exploitation, and serves as propaganda for no one, might appear impractical, naive, and anachronistic to most people today. It is thus to be feared that an objective discussion of political concepts will arouse scant interest and that the desire for such a debate will meet with little understanding. Perhaps the age of discussion is coming to an end after all. When the first edition of this treatise appeared in the summer of 1923, it was generally received in such a way as to confirm these pessimistic conjectures at least in this modest case.[1] Nevertheless it would be unjust to ignore specific examples of objective criticism, and the detailed and thoughtful review of such a leading jurist as Richard Thoma in particular deserves an exhaustive reply.[2]

The utterly fantastic political aims that Thoma imputes to me at the end of his review I may surely be allowed to pass over in silence.[3] Political combinations aside, his objective argument concerns my identification of the intellectual basis of parliamentarism in an outmoded system of thought, because I regard discussion and openness as the essential principles of parliament; something of the sort may perhaps have been the definitive conception a few generations ago, but parliament today has for a long time stood on a completely different foundation. That belief in openness and discussion appears today as outmoded is also my fear. But it must then be asked, What sort of arguments or convictions are these which have given a new intellectual foundation to parliamentarism? Naturally, institutions, like people's ideas, change in the course of time. But I do not see where contemporary parliamentarism could find a new intellectual foundation if the principles of discussion and openness really are inapplicable, or how the truth and justice of parliament could still be so evident. Like every great institution, parliament presupposes certain characteristic ideas. Whoever wants to find out what these are will be forced to return to Burke, Bentham, Guizot, and John Stuart Mill.[4] He will then be forced to admit that after them, since about 1848, there have certainly been many new practical considerations but no new principled arguments.[5] In the last century, one scarcely noticed this because parliamentarism advanced at the same time and in the closest alliance with democracy, without either of them being carefully distinguished from the other.[6] But today after their common victory, the difference manifests itself and the distinction between liberal parliamentary ideas and mass democratic ideas cannot remain unnoticed any longer. Therefore one has to concern oneself with those "moldy" greats, as Thoma puts it, because what is specific to parliamentarism can only be gleaned from their thought, and only there does parliament retain the particular character of a specially founded institution that can demonstrate its intellectual superiority to direct democracy as well as Bolshevism and Fascism.[7] That the parliamentary enterprise today is the lesser evil, that it will continue to be preferable to Bolshevism and dictatorship, that it would have unforeseeable consequences were it to be discarded, that it is "socially and technically" a very practical thing—all these are interesting and in part also correct observations. But they do not constitute the intellectual foundations of a specifically intended institution. Parliamentarism exists today as a method of government and a political system. Just as everything else that exists and functions tolerably, it is useful—no more and no less. It counts for a great deal that even today it functions better than other untried methods, and that a minimum of order that is today actually at hand would be endangered by frivolous experiments. Every reasonable person would concede such arguments. But they do not carry weight in an argument about principles. Certainly no one would be so un-demanding that he regarded an intellectual foundation or a moral truth as proven by the question, What else?[8]

All specifically parliamentary arrangements and norms receive their meaning first through discussion and openness. This is especially true of the fundamental principle that is still recognized constitutionally, although practically hardly still believed in today, that the representative is independent of his constituents and party; it applies to the provisions concerning freedom of speech and immunity of representatives, the openness of parliamentary proceedings, and so forth.[9] These arrange-ments would be unintelligible if the principle of public discussion were no longer believed in. It is not as if one could ascribe other principles retrospectively and at will to an institution, and if its hitherto existing foundations collapse, just insert any sort of substitute arguments. Certainly the same institution can serve different practical purposes and thus allow various practical justifications. There is a "heterogeneity of purposes," shifts in meanings from the practical point of view, and functional changes in practical means, but there is no heterogeneity of principles. If we assume with Montesquieu, for example, that the principle of monarchy is honor,[10] then this principle cannot be foisted onto a democratic republic any more than a monarchy could be founded on the principle of open discussion. Indeed, a feeling for the specificity of principles seems to have disappeared and an unlimited substitution to have taken its place. In the review by Thoma mentioned above, that is really the basic idea of all the objections he raises to my article. But he does not reveal in any way at all, unfortunately, what the apparently so abundant new principles of parliamentarism are. He is satisfied in a short reference to mention "only the writings and speeches of Max Weber, Hugo Preuss, and Friedrich Naumann" in the years from 1917 onward.[11] What did parliamentarism mean to these German liberals and democrats struggling against the imperial political system? Essentially and most importantly it was a means for selecting political leaders, a certain way to overcome political dilettantism and to admit the best and most able to political leadership. Whether parliament actually possesses the capacity to build a political elite has since become very questionable. Today one would certainly not think so optimistically about this selection instrument; many would regard such hope as already outmoded, and the word *illusory*, which Thoma uses against Guizot, could easily be applied to these German democrats. What numerous parliaments in various European and non-European states have produced in the way of a political elite of hundreds of successive ministers justifies no great optimism. But worse and destroying almost every hope, in a few states, parliamentarism has already produced a situation in which all public business has become an object of spoils and compromise for the parties and their followers, and politics, far from being the concern of an elite, has become the despised business of a rather dubious class of persons.

For a principled reflection, that is still not decisive. Whoever believes that parliamentarism guarantees the best selection of political leaders remains convinced of that, at least today, not because of idealistic belief, but rather as a practical-technical hypothesis constructed on the English model, intended for application on the Continent, which one could reasonably discard if it did not succeed.[12] Nevertheless, this conviction can also be linked to belief in discussion and openness, and then it belongs to principled arguments for parliamentarism. Parliament is in any case only "true" as long as public discussion is taken seriously and implemented. "Discussion" here has a particular meaning and does not simply mean negotiation. Whoever characterizes every possible kind of deliberation and agreement as parliamentarism and everything else as dictatorship or tyranny—as M. J. Bonn does in his *Die Krisis der europäischen Demokratie*[13] and also Richard Thoma in the review mentioned above—avoids the real question. At every diplomatic conference, in every congress of delegates, in every board of directors, deliberation goes on, just as it does between the cabinets of absolute monarchs, between corporations, between Christian and Turk. The modern institution of parliament does not arise from these. One should not dissolve concepts and ignore the specific qualities of discussion. Discussion means an exchange of opinion that is governed by the purpose of persuading one's opponent through argument of the truth or justice of something, or allowing oneself to be persuaded of something as true and just. Gentz—in this matter still instructed by the liberal Burke—puts it well: The characteristic of all representative constitutions (he meant modern parliament in contrast to corporative representation or the estates) is that laws arise out of a conflict of opinions (not out of a struggle of interests).[14] To discussion belong shared convictions as premises, the willingness to be persuaded, independence of party ties, freedom from selfish interests. Most people today would regard such disinterestedness as scarcely possible. But even this skepticism belongs to the crisis of parliamentarism. The features just mentioned, which still officially belong to parliamentary constitutions, make quite clear that all specifically parliamentary arrangements assume this particular concept of discussion. The universally repeated maxim, for example, that every member of parliament is the representative, not of a party, but of the whole people and is in no way bound by instructions (repeated in article 21 of the Weimar constitution) and the recurring guarantees of freedom of speech and public sittings only make sense in terms of a correct understanding of discussion.[15] By contrast conduct that is not concerned with discovering what is rationally correct, but with calculating particular interests and the chances of winning and with carrying these through according to one's own interests is also directed by all sorts of speeches and declarations. But these are not discussions in the specific sense. When two businessmen have agreed after a trade rivalry to talk about mutual business opportunities, both have an eye naturally on their own profits, but they can still arrive at a businesslike compromise. Openness is just as inappropriate in this kind of deliberation as it is reasonable in a real discussion. There has been deliberation and compromise, as has already been noted, everywhere in world history. People know that it is better most of the time to tolerate one another than to quarrel and that a thin settlement is better than a thick lawsuit. That is without a doubt true, but it is not the principle of a specific kind of state or form of government.

The situation of parliamentarism is critical today because the development of modern mass democracy has made argumentative public discussion an empty formality. Many norms of contemporary parliamentary law, above all provisions concerning the independence of representatives and the openness of sessions, function as a result like a superfluous decoration, useless and even embarrassing, as though someone had painted the radiator of a modern central heating system with red flames in order to give the appearance of a blazing fire. The parties (which according to the text of the written constitution officially do not exist) do not face each other today discussing opinions, but as social or economic power-groups calculating their mutual interests and opportunities for power, and they actually agree compromises and coalitions on this basis. The masses are won over through a propaganda apparatus whose maximum effect relies on an appeal to immediate interests and passions. Argument in the real sense that is characteristic for genuine discussion ceases. In its place there appears a conscious reckoning of interests and chances for power in the parties' negotiations; in the treatment of the masses, posterlike, insistent suggestion or—as Walter Lippmann says in his very shrewd, although too psychological, American book *Public Opinion*—the "symbol" appears.[16] The literature on the psychology, technique, and critique of public opinion is today very large.[17] One may therefore assume as well known today that it is no longer a question of persuading one's opponent of the truth or justice of an opinion but rather of winning a majority in order to govern with it. What Cavour identified as the great distinction between absolutism and constitutional regimes, that in an absolute regime a minister gives orders, whereas in a constitutional one he persuades all those who should obey, must today be meaningless. Cavour says explicitly: I (as constitutional minister) persuade that I am right, and it is only in this connection that his famous saying is meant: "The worst chamber is still preferable to the best antechamber."[18] Today parliament itself appears a gigantic antechamber in front of the bureaus or committees of invisible rulers. It is like a satire if one quotes Bentham today: "In Parliament ideas meet, and contact between ideas gives off sparks and leads to evidence."[19] Who still remembers the time when Prévost-Paradol saw the value of parliamentarism over the "personal regime" of Napoléon III in that through the transfer of real power it forced the true holders of power to reveal themselves, so that government, as a result of this, always represents the strongest power in a "wonderful" coordination of appearance and reality?[20] Who still believes in this kind of openness? And in parliament as its greatest "platform"?

The arguments of Burke, Bentham, Guizot, and John Stuart Mill are thus antiquated today. The numerous definitions of parliamentarism which one still finds today in Anglo-Saxon and French writings and which are apparently little known in Germany, definitions in which parliamentarism appears as essentially "government by discussion,"[21] must accordingly also count as moldy. Never mind. If someone still believes in parliamentarism, he will at least have to offer new arguments for it. A reference to Friedrich Naumann, Hugo Preuss, and Max Weber is no longer sufficient. With all respect for these men, no one today would share their hope that parliament alone guarantees the education of a political elite. Such convictions have in fact been shaken and they can only remain standing today as an idealistic belief so long as they can bind themselves to belief in discussion and openness. What has been advanced during the last decades as new justifications for parliamentarism still only asserts that in our time parliament functions well or at least tolerably as a useful, even an indispensable, instrument of social and political technique. This is, just to affirm it once again, a completely plausible kind of observation. But one still has to take an interest in the deeper foundations of something Montesquieu called the principle of a state or governmental form, in the specific conviction that belongs to this as to every great institution, in the belief in parliament which once actually existed and which one no longer finds today.

In the history of political ideas, there are epochs of great energy and times becalmed, times of motionless status quo. Thus the epoch of monarchy is at an end when a sense of the principle of kingship, of honor, has been lost, if bourgeois kings appear who seek to prove their usefulness and utility instead of their devotion and honor.[22] The external apparatus of monarchical institutions can remain standing very much longer after that. But in spite of it monarchy's hour has tolled. The convictions inherent in this and no other institution then appear antiquated; practical justifications for it will not be lacking, but it is only an empirical question whether men or organizations come forward who can prove themselves just as useful or even more so than these kings and through this simple fact brush aside monarchy. The same holds true of the "social-technical" justifications for parliament. If parliament should change from an institution of evident truth into a simply practical-technical means, then it only has to be shown *via facta*, through some kind of experience, not even necessarily through an open, self-declared dictatorship, that things could be otherwise and parliament is then finished.

The belief in parliamentarism, in government by discussion, belongs to the intellectual world of liberalism. It does not belong to democracy. Both, liberalism and democracy, have to be distinguished from one another so that the patchwork picture that makes up modern mass democracy can be recognized.

Every actual democracy rests on the principle that not only are equals equal but unequals will not be treated equally.[23] Democracy requires, therefore, first homogeneity and second—if the need arises— elimination or eradication of heterogeneity.[24] To illustrate this principle it is sufficient to name two different examples of modern democracy: contemporary Turkey, with its radical expulsion of the Greeks and its reckless Turkish nationalization of the country,[25] and the Australian commonwealth, which restricts unwanted entrants through its immigration laws, and like other dominions only takes emigrants who conform to the notion of a "right type of settler."[26] A democracy demonstrates its political power by knowing how to refuse or keep at bay something foreign and unequal that threatens its homogeneity. The question of equality is precisely not one of abstract, logical-arithmetical games. It is about the substance of equality. It can be found in certain physical and moral qualities, for example, in civic virtue, in *arete*, the classical democracy of *vertus* (*vertu*). In the democracy of English sects during the seventeenth century equality was based on a consensus of religious convictions.[27] Since the nineteenth century it has existed above all in membership in a particular nation, in national homogeneity.[28] Equality is only interesting and valuable politically so long as it has substance, and for that reason at least the possibility and the risk of inequality. There may be isolated examples perhaps for the idyllic case of a community in which relationship itself is sufficient, where each of its inhabitants possesses this happy independence equally and each one is so similar to every other one physically, psychically, morally, and economically that a homogeneity without heterogeneity exists, something that was possible in primitive agrarian democracies or for a long time in the colonial states. Finally one has to say that a democracy—because inequality always belongs to equality—can exclude one part of those governed without ceasing to be a democracy, that until now people who in some way were completely or partially without rights and who were restricted from the exercise of political power, let them be called barbarians, uncivilized, atheists, aristocrats, counterrevolutionaries, or even slaves, have belonged to a democracy. Neither in the Athenian city democracy nor in the British Empire are all inhabitants of the state territory politically equal. Of the more than four hundred million inhabitants of the British Empire more than three hundred million are not British citizens. If English democracy, universal suffrage, or universal equality is spoken of, then these hundreds of millions in English democracy are just as unquestionably ignored as were slaves in Athenian democracy. Modern imperialism has created countless new governmental forms, conforming to economic and technical developments, which extend themselves to the same degree that democracy develops within the motherland. Colonies, protectorates, mandates, intervention treaties, and similar forms of dependence make it possible today for a democracy to govern a heterogeneous population without making them citizens, making them dependent upon a democratic state, and at the same time held apart from this state. That is the political and constitutional meaning of the nice formula "the colonies are foreign in public law, but domestic in international law." Current usage, that is, the vocabulary of the Anglo-Saxon world press, which Richard Thoma submits to and even accepts as the standard for a theoretical definition, ignores all of that. For him apparently every state in which universal and equal voting rights are made "the foundation of the whole" is a democracy.[29] Does the British Empire rest on universal and equal voting rights for all of its inhabitants? It could not survive for a week on this foundation; with their terrible majority, the coloreds would dominate the whites. In spite of that the British Empire is a democracy. The same applies to France and the other powers.[30]

Universal and equal suffrage is only, quite reasonably, the consequence of a substantial equality within the circle of equals and does not exceed this equality. Equal rights make good sense where homogeneity exists. But the "current usage" of "universal suffrage" implies something else: Every adult person, simply as a person, should *eo ipso* be politically equal to every other person. This is a liberal, not a democratic, idea; it replaces formerly existing democracies, based on a substantial equality and homogeneity, with a democracy of mankind. This democracy of mankind does not exist anywhere in the world today. If for no other reason than because the earth is divided into states, and indeed mostly into nationally homogeneous states, which try to develop democracy internally on the basis of national homogeneity and which, besides that, in no way treat every person as an equally entitled citizen.[31] Even a democratic state, let us say the United States of America, is far from allowing foreigners to share in its power or its wealth. Until now there has never been a democracy that did not recognize the concept "foreign" and that could have realized the equality of all men. If one were serious about a democracy of mankind and really wanted to make every person the equal politically of every other person, then that would be an equality in which every person took part as a consequence of birth or age and nothing else. Equality would have been robbed of its value and substance, because the specific meaning that it has as political equality, economic equality, and so forth—in short as equality in a particular sphere—would have been taken away. Every sphere has its specific equality and inequalities in fact. However great an injustice it would be not to respect the human worth of every individual, it would nevertheless be an irresponsible stupidity, leading to the worst chaos, and therefore to even worse injustice, if the specific characteristics of various spheres were not recognized. In the domain of the political, people do not face each other as abstractions, but as politically interested and politically determined persons, as citizens, governors or governed, politically allied or opponents—in any case, therefore, in political categories. In the sphere of the political, one cannot abstract out what is political, leaving only universal human equality; the same applies in the realm of economics, where people are not conceived as such, but as producers, consumers, and so forth, that is, in specifically economic categories.

An absolute human equality, then, would be an equality understood only in terms of itself and without risk; it would be an equality without the necessary correlate of inequality, and as a result conceptually and practically meaningless, an indifferent equality. Now, such an equality certainly does not exist anywhere, so long as the various states of the earth, as was said above, distinguish their citizens politically from other persons and exclude politically dependent populations that are unwanted, on whatever grounds, by combining dependence in international law with the definition of such populations as alien in public law. In contrast it appears that at least inside the different modern democratic states universal human equality has been established; although there is of course no absolute equality of all persons, since foreigners and aliens remain excluded, there is nevertheless a relatively far-reaching human equality among the citizenry. But it must be noted that in this case national homogeneity is usually that much more strongly emphasized, and that general human equality is once again neutralized through the definitive exclusion of all those who do not belong to the state, of those who remain outside it. Where that is not the case, where a state wants to establish general human equality in the political sphere without concern for national or some other sort of homogeneity, then it cannot escape the consequence that political equality will be devalued to the extent that it approximates absolute human equality. And not only that. The sphere of the political and therefore politics itself would also be devalued in at least the same degree, and would become something insignificant. One would not only have robbed political equality of its substance and made it meaningless for individual equals, but politics would also have become insubstantial to the extent that such an indifferent equality is taken seriously. Matters that are dealt with by the methods of an empty equality would also become insignificant. Substantive inequalities would in no way disappear from the world and the state; they would shift into another sphere, perhaps separated from the political and concentrated in the economic, leaving this area to take on a new, disproportionately decisive importance. Under conditions of superficial political equality, another sphere in which substantial inequalities prevail (today, for example, the economic sphere) will dominate politics. This is completely unavoidable and any reflection on political theory recognizes it as the real grounds for the much-deplored dominance of economics over state and politics. Wherever an indifferent concept of equality, without the necessary correlate of inequality, actually takes hold of an area of human life, then this area loses its substance and is overshadowed by another sphere in which inequality then comes into play with ruthless power.

The equality of all persons as persons is not democracy but a certain kind of liberalism, not a state form but an individualistic-humanitarian ethic and *Weltanschauung*.[32] Modern mass democracy rests on the confused combination of both. Despite all the work on Rousseau and despite the correct realization that Rousseau stands at the beginning of modern democracy, it still seems to have gone unnoticed that the theory of the state set out in *Du Contrat social* contains these two different elements incoherently next to each other.[33] The façade is liberal: the state's legitimacy is justified by a free contract. But the subsequent depiction and the development of the central concept, the "general will," demonstrates that a true state, according to Rousseau, only exists where the people are so homogeneous that there is essentially unanimity. According to the *Contrat social* there can be no parties in the state, no special interests, no religious differences, nothing that can divide persons, not even a public financial concern. This philosopher of modern democracy, respected by significant national economists such as Alfred Weber[34] and Carl Brinkmann,[35] says in all seriousness: finance is something for slaves, a *mot d'esclave*.[36] It should be noticed that for Rousseau the word *slave* has an entirely consequential meaning attained in the construction of the democratic state; it signifies those who do not belong to the people, the unequal, the alien or noncitizen who is not helped by the fact that *in abstracto* he is a "person," the heterogeneous, who does not participate in the general homogeneity and is therefore rightly excluded from it. According to Rousseau this unanimity must go so far that the laws come into existence *sans discussion*. Even judges and parties in a suit must want the same,[37] whereby it is never even asked which of the two parties, accused or accuser, wants the same. In short, homogeneity elevated into an identity understands itself completely from itself. But if unanimity and agreement of all wills with one another is really so great, why then must another contract be concluded or even construed? A contract assumes differences and oppositions. Unanimity, just like the general will, is either there or not and it may even be, as Alfred Weber has accurately pointed out, naturally present.[38] Where it exists a contract is meaningless. Where it does not exist, a contract does not help. The idea of a free contract of all with all comes from a completely different theoretical world where opposing interests, differences, and egoisms are assumed. This idea comes from liberalism. The general will as Rousseau constructs it is in truth homogeneity. That is a really consequential democracy. According to the *Contrat social*, the state therefore rests not on a contract but essentially on homogeneity, in spite of its title and in spite of the dominant contract theory. The democratic identity of governed and governing arises from that.

The state theory of the *Contrat social* also proves that democracy is correctly defined as the identity of governed and governing. When it has been noticed, this definition,[39] which appears in my *Politische Theologie* (1922) and in the article on parliamentarism, was partially rejected and partially taken over. Here I would like to mention that while its application to contemporary state theory and its extension to a new range of identities are new, it is ultimately an ancient, one can even say classical, definition that conforms to a tradition that is for these reasons no longer well known. Because of its reference to interesting and particularly urgent consequences in public law today, Pufendorf's formulation should be quoted:[40] In a democracy, where those who command and those who obey are identical, the sovereign, that is, an assembly composed of all citizens, can change laws and change constitutions at will; in a monarchy or aristocracy, "where there are some who command and some who are commanded," a mutual contract is possible, according to Pufendorf, and thus also a limitation of state power.

A popular presentation sees parliamentarism in the middle today, threatened from both sides by Bolshevism and Fascism. That is a simple but superficial constellation. The crisis of the parliamentary system and of parliamentary institutions in fact springs from the circumstances of modern mass democracy. These lead first of all to a crisis of democracy itself, because the problem of a substantial equality and homogeneity, which is necessary to democracy, cannot be resolved by the general equality of mankind. It leads further to a crisis of parliamentarism that must certainly be distinguished from the crisis of democracy. Both crises have appeared today at the same time and each one aggravates the other, but they are conceptually and in reality different. As democracy, modern mass democracy attempts to realize an identity of governed and governing, and thus it confronts parliament as an inconceivable and outmoded institution. If democratic identity is taken seriously, then in an emergency, no other constitutional institution can withstand the sole criterion of the people's will, however it is expressed. Against the will of the people especially an institution based on discussion by independent representatives has no autonomous justification for its existence, even less so because the belief in discussion is not democratic but originally liberal. Today one can distinguish three crises: the crisis of democracy (M. J. Bonn directs his attention to this without noticing the contradiction between liberal notions of human equality and democratic homogeneity); further, a crisis of the modern state (Alfred Weber); and finally a crisis of parliamentarism.[41] The crisis of parliamentarism presented here rests on the fact that democracy and liberalism could be allied to each other for a time, just as socialism and democracy have been allied; but as soon as it achieves power, liberal democracy must decide between its elements, just as social democracy, which is finally in fact a social-liberal democracy inasmuch as modern mass democracy contains essentially liberal elements, must also decide. In democracy there is only the equality of equals, and the will of those who belong to the equals. All other institutions transform themselves into insubstantial social-technical expedients which are not in a position to oppose the will of the people, however expressed, with their own values and their own principles. The crisis of the modern state arises from the fact that no state can realize a mass democracy, a democracy of mankind, not even a democratic state.

Bolshevism and Fascism by contrast are, like all dictatorships, certainly antiliberal but not necessarily antidemocratic. In the history of democracy there have been numerous dictatorships, Caesarisms, and other more striking forms that have tried to create homogeneity and to shape the will of the people with methods uncommon in the liberal tradition of the past century. This effort belongs to the undemocratic conception, resulting from a blend of liberal principles in the nineteenth century that a people could only express its will when each citizen voted in deepest secrecy and complete isolation, that is, without leaving the sphere of the private and irresponsible, under "protective arrangements" and "unobserved"—as required by Reich voting law in Germany.[42] Then every single vote was registered and an arithmetical majority was calculated. Quite elementary truths have thus been lost and are apparently unknown in contemporary political theory. "The people" is a concept in public law.[43] The people exist only in the sphere of publicity. The unanimous opinion of one hundred million private persons is neither the will of the people nor public opinion. The will of the people can be expressed just as well and perhaps better through acclamation, through something taken for granted, an obvious and unchallenged presence, than through the statistical apparatus that has been constructed with such meticulousness in the last fifty years. The stronger the power of democratic feeling, the more certain is the awareness that democracy is something other than a registration system for secret ballots. Compared to a democracy that is direct, not only in the technical sense but also in a vital sense, parliament appears an artificial machinery, produced by liberal reasoning, while dictatorial and Caesaristic methods not only can produce the acclamation of the people but can also be a direct expression of democratic substance and power.

Even if Bolshevism is suppressed and Fascism held at bay, the crisis of contemporary parliamentarism would not be overcome in the least. For it has not appeared as a result of the appearance of those two opponents; it was there before them and will persist after them. Rather, the crisis springs from the consequences of modern mass democracy and in the final analysis from the contradiction of a liberal individualism burdened by moral pathos and a democratic sentiment governed essentially by political ideals. A century of historical alliance and common struggle against royal absolutism has obscured the awareness of this contradiction. But the crisis unfolds today ever more strikingly, and no cosmopolitan rhetoric can prevent or eliminate it. It is, in its depths, the inescapable contradiction of liberal individualism and democratic homogeneity.

Introduction to the
First Edition (1923)

As long as parliamentarism has existed, there has also been a literature criticizing it.[1] It was first developed, understandably, on the ground of reaction and restoration by political opponents who were defeated in the struggle against parliamentarism. Increasing practical experience brought out the deficiencies of party government, and these were then given prominence. Finally, a critique came from another principled side, from the radicalism of the left. Thus, right-wing and left-wing tendencies, conservative, syndicalist, and anarchist arguments, and monarchist, aristocratic, and democratic perspectives here joined forces. One finds the simplest summary of the current situation in a speech that Senator Mosca made in the Italian Senate on November 26, 1922, concerning the domestic and foreign policy of Mussolini's government.[2] According to Mosca, three radical solutions offer themselves as a corrective for the deficiencies of the parliamentary system: the so-called dictatorship of the proletariat; a return to the more or less disguised absolutism of a bureaucracy ("un assolutismo burocratico"); and, finally, a form of syndicalist government, that is, replacing the individualistic representation that exists in contemporary parliament with an organization of syndicates. The last was regarded by the speaker as the greatest danger to the parliamentary system because syndicalism springs, not from doctrines and feelings, but from the economic organization of modern society. Henry Berthélemy, by contrast, who expressed himself on the matter in his preface to the tenth edition of his *Traité élémentaire de droit administratif*, does not consider syndicalism worth talking about. He believes that it is sufficient if parliamentarians recognize the danger in a confusion of powers, give up their party business, and provide for a certain stability in administration. Finally, he views regionalism as well as industrialism (the application of the methods of economic life to politics) as a danger to the state, while saying about syndicalism that one could not take seriously a theory that believed that everything would fall into order "if authority comes from those over whom it is exercised, and if the control is entrusted precisely to those who must be controlled."[3] From the standpoint of a good bureaucratic administration this is quite right, but what does it imply for democratic theory, the theory that all governmental authority derives from the governed?

In Germany there has long been a tradition of corporatist ideas and currents for which the critique of modern parliamentarism is nothing new. A literature has developed parallel to it in the last few years concerned with everyday experiences since 1919. In numerous brochures and newspaper articles, the most prominent deficiencies and mistakes of the parliamentary enterprise have been pointed out: the dominance of parties, their unprofessional politics of personalities, "the government of amateurs," continuing governmental crises, the purposelessness and banality of parliamentary debate, the declining standard of parliamentary customs, the destructive methods of parliamentary obstruction, the misuse of parliamentary immunities and privileges by a radical opposition which is contemptuous of parliamentarism itself, the undignified daily order of business, the poor attendance in the House. The impression based on long familiar observations has gradually spread: that proportional representation and the list system destroy the relationship between voters and representatives, make fractions an indispensable means of government in parliament, and make the so-called representative principle (article 21 of the Reich constitution states that "the members are representatives of the whole people, they are only responsible to their own consciences and not bound to any instructions") meaningless; further, that the real business takes place, not in the open sessions of a plenum, but in committees and not even necessarily in parliamentary committees, and that important decisions are taken in secret meetings of faction leaders or even in extraparliamentary committees so that responsibility is transferred and even abolished, and in this way the whole parliamentary system finally becomes only a poor façade concealing the dominance of parties and economic interests.[4] In addition to that critique there is also a critique of the democratic foundations of this parliamentary system that was more natural in the middle of the nineteenth century. It developed from the classical tradition of Western European education and the fear that the educated had of dominance by the uneducated masses, a fear of democracy whose typical expression one finds in the letters of Jacob Burckhardt.[5] In its place there has long since developed an investigation of the methods and techniques with which the parties create electoral propaganda, persuade the masses, and dominate public opinion. Ostrogorski's work on the parties in modern democracy is typical of this kind of literature; Belloc and Chesterton's *Party System* made the critique popular; sociological investigations of party life, mostly the famous book by Robert Michels, destroyed numerous parliamentary and democratic illusions without separating one from the other.[6] Finally, even nonsocialists recognized the collusion of press, party, and capital and treated politics only as a shadow of economic reality.

One can assume that this literature is generally well known. The scholarly interest of the following investigation is not intended either to confirm or to refute it; it is rather an attempt to find the ultimate core of the institution of modern parliament. Accordingly it will be shown that the systematic basis from which modern parliamentarism developed is scarcely discernible in the terms of current political and social thought, and how far the institution itself has lost its moral and intellectual foundation and only remains standing through sheer mechanical perseverance as an empty apparatus. Only when they grasp the situation intellectually could reform proposals gain perspective. Concepts such as democracy, liberalism, individualism, and rationalism, all of which are used in connection with modern parliament, must be more clearly distinguished so that they cease to be provisional characterizations and slogans. Only then can there be a shift away from tactical and technical questions to intellectual principles and a starting point that does not once again lead to a dead end.

1

Democracy and Parliamentarism

The history of political and state theory in the nineteenth century could be summarized with a single phrase: the triumphal march of democracy.[1] No state in the Western European cultural world withstood the extension of democratic ideas and institutions. Even where powerful social forces defended themselves, such as in the Prussian monarchy, no intellectual force that could have defeated democratic beliefs reached outside its own circle of adherents. Progress and the extension of democracy were equated, and the antidemocratic resistance was considered an empty defense, the protection of historically outmoded things and a struggle of the old with the new. Every epoch of political and state thought has conceptions which appear evident to it in a specific sense and, even if also with many misunderstandings and mythologizing, are, without anything further, plausible to great masses. In the nineteenth century and into the twentieth, this kind of obviousness and evidence was certainly on the side of democracy. Ranke called the idea of popular sovereignty the most powerful conception of the age, and its conflict with the principle of monarchy the dominant current of the century.[2] Since then this conflict has ended in the victory of democracy.

Since the 1830s all major French thinkers with a sense of intellectual trends have believed increasingly that Europe must, in an unavoidable destiny, become democratic. This was most profoundly felt and expressed by Alexis de Tocqueville.[3] Guizot was also guided by this idea, although he was also afraid of democratic chaos. The dispensation of providence appeared to have decided in favor of democracy. There was a frequently repeated image of this: the flood of democracy, against which there seemed to have been no dam since 1789. The most impressive description of this development, given by Taine in his English literary history, was formed under Guizot's influence.[4] One judged the development in various ways: Tocqueville with an aristocratic fear of bourgeois mankind, the "collection of timid and industrious animals"; Guizot hoped to tame this terrible force; Michelet had an enthusiastic belief in the natural goodness of "the people"; Renan felt the disgust of the educated and the skepticism of a historian; and the socialists were convinced that they were the true heirs of democracy. It is proof of the remarkable self-evidence of democratic ideas that even socialism, which appeared as the new idea of the nineteenth century, decided in favor of an alliance with democracy. Many had tried to form a coalition between democracy and the established monarchies because the liberal bourgeoisie was a common enemy of conservative monarchy and the proletarian masses. This tactical cooperation expressed itself in different alliances and even enjoyed some success in England under Disraeli,[5] but in the last analysis it worked again to the advantage of democracy alone. In Germany there remained in this respect pious wishes and a "romantic socialism." The socialist organization of the mass of workers here took over progressive-democratic ideas so exactly that they appeared to be the protagonists of these ideas in Germany, far outstripping bourgeois democrats; and they had the double task of realizing both socialist and democratic demands at the same time.[6] One could regard both as identical, because one believed they constituted progress and the future.

Thus democracy appeared to have the self-evidence of an irresistible advancing and expanding force. So long as it was essentially a polemical concept (that is, the negation of established monarchy), democratic convictions could be joined to and reconciled with various other political aspirations. But to the extent that it was realized, democracy was seen to serve many masters and not in any way to have a substantial, clear goal. As its most important opponent, the monarchical principle, disappeared, democracy itself lost its substantive precision and shared the fate of every polemical concept. At first, democracy appeared in an entirely obvious alliance, even identity, with liberalism and freedom. In social democracy it joined with socialism. The success of Napoleon III and the results of Swiss referenda demonstrate that it could actually be conservative and reactionary, just as Proudhon prophesied.[7] If all political tendencies could make use of democracy, then this proved that it had no political content and was only an organizational form; and if one regarded it from the perspective of some political program that one hoped to achieve with the help of democracy, then one had to ask oneself what value democracy itself had merely as a form. The attempt to give democracy a content by transferring it from the political to the economic sphere did not answer the question. Such transferences from the political into the economic are to be found in numerous publications. English guild socialism calls itself economic democracy; a well-known analogy of the constitutional state with constitutional factories has been extended in every possible direction.[8] In truth this signifies an essential change in the concept of democracy because a political point of view cannot be transferred into economic relationships as long as freedom of contract and civil law hold sway in the economy. Max Weber had already argued in his article "Parliament und Regierung im neugeordneten Deutschland" (1918) that the state was sociologically just another large business and that an economic administrative system, a factory, and the state are today no longer essentially different.[9] From that Kelsen drew the conclusion, perhaps too soon, in his work *Wesen und Wert der Demokratie* (1921) that "for that reason organizational problems are fundamentally the same in both cases, and democracy is a question not only of the state but also of commercial enterprises."[10] But a political form of organization ceases to be political if it is, like the modern economy, based on private law. There are certainly analogies between a monarch, the absolute master in the state, and a capitalist, who (naturally in a completely different sense) is the absolute master in his business. There are possibilities on both sides for participation by the subordinates, but the form and content of authority, publicity, and representation are essentially different. Finally, it would also contradict every rule of economic thought to apply by way of analogy political forms which have been created on very different assumptions to modern economic conditions, or, to use a well-known economic image, to transfer the construction of a superstructure onto an essentially different substructure.

The various nations or social and economic groups who organize themselves "democratically" have the same subject, 'the people', only in the abstract. *In concreto* the masses are sociologically and psychologically heterogeneous. A democracy can be militarist or pacifist, absolutist or liberal, centralized or decentralized, progressive or reactionary, and again different at different times without ceasing to be a democracy. From these facts it stands to reason that one cannot give democracy content by means of a transfer into the economic sphere. What remains then of democracy? For its definition, one has a string of identities. It belongs to the essence of democracy that every and all decisions which are taken are only valid for those who themselves decide. That the outvoted minority must be ignored in this only causes theoretical and superficial difficulties. In reality even this rests on the identity that constantly recurs in democratic logic and on the essential democratic argument—as will be seen immediately— that the will of the outvoted minority is in truth identical with the will of the majority. Rousseau's frequently cited arguments in *Contrat social* are fundamental for democratic thought and ultimately conform to an ancient tradition.[11] It is to be found almost literally in Locke:[12]

In democracy the citizen even agrees to the law that is against his own will, for the law is the General Will and, in turn, the will of the free citizen. Thus a citizen never really gives his consent to a specific content but rather *in abstracto* to the result that evolves out of the general will, and he votes only so that the votes out of which one can know this general will can be calculated. If the result deviates from the intention of those individuals voting, then the outvoted know that they have mistaken the content of the general will: "This only proves that I have made a mistake, and that what I believed to be the General Will, was not so."[13] And because, as Rousseau emphatically continues, the general will conforms to true freedom, then the outvoted were not free. With this Jacobin logic one can, it is well known, justify the rule of a minority over the majority, even while appealing to democracy. But the essence of the democratic principle is preserved, namely, the assertion of an identity between law and the people's will. For an abstract logic it really makes no difference whether one identifies the will of the majority or the will of the minority with the will of the people if it can never be the absolutely unanimous will of all citizens (including those not eligible to vote).

If the franchise is given to an increasing number of people in an ever-broader extension, then that is a symptom of the endeavor to realize the identity between state and people; at its basis there is a particular conception about the preconditions on which one accepts this identity as real. But that does not change anything about the fundamental conception that all democratic arguments rest logically on a series of identities. In this series belong the identity of governed and governing, sovereign and subject, the identity of the subject and object of state authority, the identity of the people with their representatives in parliament, the identity of the state and the current voting population, the identity of the state and the law, and finally an identity of the quantitative (the numerical majority or unanimity) with the qualitative (the justice of the laws).

All of these identities are not palpable reality, but rest on a recognition of the identity. It is not a matter of something actually equal legally, politically, or sociologically, but rather of identifications. Extension of the suffrage, the reduction of electoral terms of office, the introduction and extension of referenda and initiatives—in short, everything that one identifies as an institution of direct democracy or a tendency toward it and all those things which, as has just been mentioned, are governed by the notion of an identity—are in consequence democratic. But they can never reach an absolute, direct identity that is actually present at every moment. A distance always remains between real equality and the results of identification. The will of the people is of course always identical with the will of the people, whether a decision comes from the yes or no of millions of voting papers, or from a single individual who has the will of the people even without a ballot, or from the people acclaiming in some way. Everything depends on how the will of the people is formed. The ancient dialectic in the theory of the will of the people has still not been resolved: The minority might express the true will of the people; the people can be deceived, and one has long been familiar with the techniques of propaganda and the manipulation of public opinion. This dialectic is as old as democracy itself and does not in any way begin with Rousseau or the Jacobins. Even at the beginning of modern democracy one comes across the remarkable contradiction that the radical democrats understood their democratic radicalism as a selection criterion that distinguished them from others as the true representatives of the people's will. From this there arose in practice an extremely undemocratic exclusivity, because only the representatives of true democracy were granted political rights. At the same time a new aristocracy emerged. It is an old sociological phenomenon that repeats itself in every revolution; it did not appear first with the November socialists of 1918, but showed itself everywhere in 1848 in those who were called "old republicans."[14] It is entirely consistent to maintain that democracy can only be introduced for a people who really think democratically. The first direct democracy of the modern period, the Levellers of the Puritan Revolution, were not able to escape this democratic dialectic. Their leader Lilburne wrote in his *Legal Fundamental Principles of the People of England* (1649) that only the "well-affected" should have voting rights, that the elected representatives of these "well-affected" people must have legislative power completely in their hands, and that the constitution must be a contract signed by the "well-affected."[15]

Democracy seems fated then to destroy itself in the problem of the formation of a will. For radical democrats, democracy as such has its own value without reference to the content of the politics pursued with the help of democracy. If the danger exists that democracy might be used in order to defeat democracy,[16] then the radical democrat has to decide whether to remain a democrat against the majority or to give up his own position. As soon as democracy takes on the content of a self-sufficient value, then one can no longer remain (in the formal sense) a democrat at any price. It is a remarkable fact and a necessity, but in no way an abstract dialectic or sophistical game.[17] It often happens that democrats are in the minority. It also happens that they decide on the basis of a supposedly democratic principle in favor of women's suffrage and then have the experience that the majority of women do not vote democratically. Then the familiar program of "people's education" unfolds: The people can be brought to recognize and express their own will correctly through the right education. This means nothing else but that the educator identifies his will at least provisionally with that of the people, not to mention that the content of the education that the pupil will receive is also decided by the educator. The consequence of this educational theory is a dictatorship that suspends democracy in the name of a true democracy that is still to be created. Theoretically, this does not destroy democracy, but it is important to pay attention to it because it shows that dictatorship is not antithetical to democracy. Even during a transitional period dominated by the dictator, a democratic identity can still exist and the will of the people can still be the exclusive criterion. It is then particularly noticeable that the single practical question affected is the question of identification, and specifically the question of who has control over the means with which the will of the people is to be constructed: military and political force, propaganda, control of public opinion through the press, party organizations, assemblies, popular education, and schools. In particular, only political power, which should come from the people's will, can form the people's will in the first place.

One can say today, faced with the expansion of democratic thought, that an identity with the will of the people has become so common a premise that it has ceased to be politically interesting, and that the conflict only concerns the means of identification. It would be foolish to deny a generally accepted agreement here. Not only because today there are no kings who have the courage to declare openly that if necessary they would remain on the throne against the will of the people, but also because every significant political power can hope by some means to achieve this identification one day. For that reason none has an interest in denying a democratic identity. On the contrary, all are more interested in knowing how to confirm it.

The rule of the Bolshevist government in Soviet Russia certainly counts as a notable example of disregard for democratic principles. Nevertheless, its theoretical argument remains within the democratic current (with exceptions that will be mentioned in chapter 4) and only uses modern criticism and modern experiences of the misuse of political democracy. What counts as democracy in Western European states today is for them only the trickery of capital's economic dominance over press and parties, that is, the lie of a falsely educated popular will. Communism would be the first true democracy. Apart from its economic foundations, this is, in its structure, the old Jacobin argument. From the opposite side, a royalist publicist can express his contempt for democracy with the tenet: Prevailing public opinion today is so stupid that with the correct approach it could be brought to renounce its own power. This means that it could be brought "to demand an act of common sense from something that lacks sense—but isn't it always possible to find absurd motives for an act which is not in itself at all absurd?"[18] There is mutual agreement on this on both sides. When the theorists of Bolshevism suspend democracy in the name of true democracy and the enemies of democracy hope to deceive it, then the one still assumes that democratic principles are theoretically correct, and the other that it is democracy's real supremacy that has to be reckoned with. Only Italian Fascism seems to place no value on being "democratic." With that exception one must say that until now the democratic principle has been universally accepted without contradiction.

That is significant for the jurisprudence of public law. Neither the theory nor the practice of constitutional and international law could get along without a concept of *legitimacy* and for that reason it is important that the dominant concept of legitimacy today is in fact democratic. The development from 1815 until 1918 could be depicted as the development of a concept of legitimacy: from dynastic to democratic legitimacy. The democratic principle must today claim an importance analogous to that earlier possessed by the monarchical. This point cannot be developed here, but it must at least be said that a concept such as legitimacy cannot change its subject without also changing its structure and its content. Two different types of legitimacy exist today without the concept's ceasing to be indispensable or preserving its essential functions, even if jurists are little aware of these. Under public law every government today is in general only provisional until it has been sanctioned by an assembly based on democratic principles, and every government that does not rest on this basis appears a usurpation. One assumes (although it does not follow from the principle of democracy) that the people are indeed mature and do not any longer need a Jacobin educational dictatorship. Prevailing legal conviction today and the concept of legitimacy, which rests on the demand for a constitutional assembly, express themselves in the way one regards intervention in a state's constitutional affairs. It is regarded as a fundamental difference between the Holy Alliance and the contemporary League of Nations that the League of Nations only guarantees the external status quo of its members and refrains from intervention in their internal questions.[19] But with the same logic that led monarchical legitimacy to intervention, so too can intervention be justified by an appeal to the people's right of self-determination. In the numerous protests against the Soviet government motivated by democratic convictions, the essential presumption of the democratic principle of nonintervention, namely, that a constitution must not contradict the will of a people, is recognizable. If a constitution is imposed and democratic principles are thus violated, then the people's right to self-determination may be restored, and that happens precisely through intervention. An intervention based on the concept of monarchical legitimacy is illegal in democratic theory only because it violates the principle of the people's self-determination. By contrast a restoration of free self-determination achieved through intervention, the liberation of a people from a tyrant, cannot violate the principle of nonintervention in any way, but only creates the preconditions for the principle of nonintervention. Even a modern League of Nations based on democratic foundations needs a concept of legitimacy, and as a result of this, it also requires the possibility of intervention if the principle on which it is juridically based should be damaged.[20]

Thus, for many juridical investigations today, one can begin with democratic maxims without risking the misunderstanding of having accepted all of the definitions which constitute the political reality of democracy. Theoretically, and in critical times also practically, democracy is helpless before the Jacobin argument, that is, when faced with the authoritative identification of a minority as the people and with the decisive transfer of the concept from the quantitative into the qualitative. Interest is then directed toward the creation and shaping of the popular will, and the belief that all power comes from the people takes on a meaning similar to the belief that all authoritative power comes from God. Both maxims permit various governmental forms and juristic consequences in political reality. A scientific study of democracy must begin with a particular aspect that I have called political theology.[21] Because parliamentarism and democracy were so closely allied with each other in the nineteenth century that they could be accepted as synonymous, these comments on democracy must be made first. But democracy can exist without what one today calls parliamentarism and parliamentarism without democracy; and dictatorship is just as little the definitive antithesis of democracy as democracy is of dictatorship.

2

The Principles of
Parliamentarism

In the struggle between parliament and monarchy, a government that was decisively influenced by the representation of the people was called a parliamentary government, and the word was thus applied to a particular kind of executive. The meaning of the concept "parliamentarism" was thereby changed. "Parliamentary government" presupposes a parliament, and to demand such a government means that one begins with parliament as an existing institution in order to extend its powers, or, in the customary language of constitutionalism, the legislative should influence the executive. The fundamental concept of the parliamentary principle cannot rest solely on the participation of parliament in government, and so far as the question that interests us here is concerned, it cannot be expected that a discussion of this postulate of parliamentary government would produce much. We are concerned here with the ultimate intellectual foundations of parliamentarism itself, not with the extension of the power of parliament. Why has parliament been in fact the *ultimum sapientiae* for many generations, and on what has the belief in this institution rested for over a century? The demand that parliament must control the government, and influence the selection of ministers who are responsible to it, assumes that belief.

The oldest justification for parliament, constantly repeated through the centuries, takes into account an extreme "expedient":[1] The people in its entirety must decide, as was originally the case when all members of the community could assemble themselves under the village tree. But for practical reasons it is impossible today for everyone to come together at the same time in one place; it is also impossible to ask everyone about every detail. Because of this, one helps oneself quite reasonably with an elected committee of responsible people, and parliament is precisely that. So the familiar scale originated: Parliament is a committee of the people, the government is a committee of parliament. The notion of parliamentarism thereby appears to be something essentially democratic. But in spite of all its coincidence with democratic ideas and all the connections it has to them, parliamentarism is not democracy any more than it is realized in the practical perspective of expediency. If for practical and technical reasons the representatives of the people can decide instead of the people themselves, then certainly a single trusted representative could also decide in the name of the same people.[2] Without ceasing to be democratic, the argument would justify an antiparliamentary Caesarism. Consequently, this cannot be specific to the idea of parliamentarism, and the essential point is not that parliament is a committee of the people, a council of trusted men. There is even a contradiction here in that parliament, as the first committee, is independent of the people throughout the electoral period and is not usually subject to recall, whereas the parliamentary government, the second committee, is always dependent on the trust of the first committee and can therefore be recalled at any time.

The *ratio* of parliament rests, according to the apt characterization of Rudolf Smend,[3] in a "dynamic-dialectic," that is, in a process of confrontation of differences and opinions, from which the real political will results. The essence of parliament is therefore public deliberation of argument and counterargument, public debate and public discussion, parley, and all this without taking democracy into account.[4] The absolutely typical chain of thought is to be found in the absolutely typical representative of parliamentarism, in Guizot. Starting from right (as the opposite to might), he lists the essential characteristics of a system that guarantees the rule of law: (1) that "the powers" are always forced to discuss and thereby to seek the truth together; (2) that the openness of the whole of political life places "the powers" under the citizens' control; and (3) that press freedom prompts citizens to seek the truth for themselves and to make it known to "the powers."[5] Parliament is accordingly the place in which particles of reason that are strewn unequally among human beings gather themselves and bring public power under their control. This appears a typical rationalist idea. Nevertheless it would be incomplete and inexact to define modern parliament as an institution that has come into existence out of the rationalist spirit. Its ultimate justification and its obviousness to a whole epoch rests on the fact that this rationalism is not absolute and direct, but relative in a specific sense. Against Guizot's maxim, Mohl objected: Where is there any kind of certainty that the possessors of particles of reason are to be found precisely in parliament?[6] The answer lies in the notion of free competition and a preestablished harmony, which, certainly in the institution of parliament, as in politics itself, often appears in a hardly recognizable disguise.

It is essential that liberalism be understood as a consistent, comprehensive metaphysical system. Normally one only discusses the economic line of reasoning that social harmony and the maximization of wealth follow from the free economic competition of individuals, from freedom of contract, freedom of trade, free enterprise. But all this is only an application of a general liberal principle. It is exactly the same: That the truth can be found through an unrestrained clash of opinion and that competition will produce harmony. The intellectual core of this thought resides finally in its specific relationship to truth, which becomes a mere function of the eternal competition of opinions. In contrast to the truth, it means renouncing a definite result. In

German thought the notion of eternal discussion was more accessible in the Romantic conception of an unending conversation,[7] and it may be remarked in passing that all the intellectual confusion of the conventional reading of German political Romanticism, which characterizes it as conservative and antiliberal, is revealed in precisely this connection. Freedom of speech, freedom of press, freedom of assembly, freedom of discussion, are not only useful and expedient, therefore, but really life-and-death questions for liberalism. Guizot's description placed particular emphasis on freedom of the press as the third characteristic of parliamentarism, after discussion and openness. One can easily see that freedom of the press is only a means for discussion and openness and not an independent factor. But since a free press is a typical means for the other characteristic features of liberalism, Guizot is quite justified in giving it particular emphasis.

Only if the central place of discussion in the liberal system is correctly recognized do the two political demands that are characteristic of liberal rationalism take on their proper significance with a scientific clarity above the confused atmosphere of slogans, political tactics, and pragmatic considerations: the postulate of openness in political life and the demand for a division of powers, or more specifically the theory of a balance of opposing forces from which truth will emerge automatically as an equilibrium. Because of the decisive importance of openness and especially of the power of public opinion in liberal thought, it appears that liberalism and democracy are identical here. In the theory of the division of powers, that is obviously not the case. These, on the contrary, are used by Hasbach in order to construct the sharpest contrast between liberalism and democracy.[8] A threefold division of powers, a substantial distinction between the legislative and the executive, the rejection of the idea that the plenitude of state power should be allowed to gather at any one point—all of this is in fact the antithesis of a democratic concept of identity. The two postulates are thus not simple equivalents. Of the many very different ideas connected to these two demands, only those that are essential for the understanding of the intellectual center of modern parliamentarism will be considered here.

1 Openness

The belief in public opinion has its roots in a conception that has not been properly emphasized in the enormous literature on public opinion, not even in Tönnies's great work.[9] It is less a question of public opinion than a question about the openness of opinions. This becomes clear when one identifies the historical contradiction from which these demands arise and have arisen, namely, the theory of state secrets, *Arcana rei publicae*, that dominates much of sixteenth- and seventeenth-century literature. This theory of a great practice began with the literature on *Staatsraison*, the *ratio status* of which it is actually the core; its literary beginning is in Machiavelli and its high point in Paolo Sarpi. For a systematic and methodological treatment by German scholars, Arnold Clapmar's book can be mentioned as an example.[10] It is, generally speaking, a theory that treats the state and politics only as techniques for the assertion of power and its expansion. Against its Machiavellianism there arose a great anti-Machiavellian literature, which, shocked by the St. Bartholomew's Massacre (1572), boiled with indignation at the immorality of such principles. It answered the power ideal of political technique with the concept of law and justice. This was above all the argument of the Monarchomachian authors against princely absolutism.[11] In intellectual history this controversy is first of all only an example of the old struggle between might and right: The Machiavellian use of power is combated with a moral and legal ethos. But this description is incomplete because specific counterdemands gradually develop: precisely those two postulates of openness and the division of powers. These try to neutralize the concentration of power contained in absolutism through a system of the division of powers. The postulate of openness finds its specific opponent in the idea that *Arcana* belong to every kind of politics, political-technical secrets which are in fact just as necessary for absolutism as business and economic secrets are for an economic life that depends on private property and competition.

Cabinet politics, conducted by a few people behind closed doors, now appears something *eo ipso* evil, and as a result, the openness of political life seems to be right and good just because of its openness. Openness becomes an absolute value, although at first it was only a practical means to combat the bureaucratic, specialist-technical secret politics of absolutism. The elimination of secret politics and secret diplomacy becomes a wonder cure for every kind of political disease and corruption, and public opinion becomes a totally effective controlling force. Of course, public opinion attained this absolute character first in the eighteenth century, during the Enlightenment. The light of the public is the light of the Enlightenment, a liberation from superstition, fanaticism, and ambitious intrigue. In every system of Enlightened despotism, public opinion plays the role of an absolute corrective. The power of a despot can be all the greater as Enlightenment increases, for Enlightened public opinion makes the abuse of power impossible in itself. For the Enlightened, that can be taken for granted. Le Mercier de la Rivière developed the notion systematically.[12] Condorcet attempted to draw out its practical conclusions with an enthusiastic belief in freedom of speech and the press that is very moving when one remembers the experiences of recent generations: Where there is freedom of the press, the misuse of power is unthinkable; a single free newspaper would destroy the most powerful tyrant; the printing press is the basis of freedom, "the art that creates liberty."[13] Even Kant was in this respect only an expression of the political belief of his time, a belief in the progress of publicity and in the public's ability to enlighten itself inevitably, if it were only free to do so.[14] In England the fanatic of liberal rationality was Jeremy Bentham. Before him, argument in England had been essentially practical and pragmatic. Bentham proclaimed the significance of a free press from a liberal ideology: Freedom of public discussion, especially freedom of the press, is the most effective protection against political abuses, and "controlling power" is the real "check to arbitrary power" and so forth.[15] As this idea developed one comes across its contradiction of democracy once more. John Stuart Mill understood, with despairing concern, that a contradiction between democracy and freedom is possible and that the majority could crush minorities. Even the thought that a single person might be deprived of the opportunity to express his opinion set this positivist in an inexplicable uproar, because he considered it possible that this individual's expression of opinion might have come closest to the truth.[16]

Public opinion protected through freedom of speech, freedom of the press, freedom of assembly, and parliamentary immunities means freedom of opinion in liberal thought, with all the significance which the word *freedom* has in this system. Where the public can exercise pressure—through a single individual casting a vote, for example— here, at the transition of the private into the public, the contradictory demand for a secret ballot appears. Freedom of opinion is a freedom for private people; it is necessary for that competition of opinions in which the best opinion wins.

2 The division (balance) of powers

In modern parliamentarism the belief in public opinion is bound to a second, more organizational conception: the division or balance of different state activities and institutions. Here too the idea of competition appears, a competition from which the truth will emerge. That parliament assumes the role of the legislative in the division of powers and is limited to that role makes the rationalism which is at the heart of the theory of a balance of powers rather relative and, as will now be shown, it distinguishes this system from the absolute rationalism of the Enlightenment. One does not need to waste many words on the general meaning of the idea of balance. Of the images which typically recur in the history of political thought and state theory, and whose systematic investigation has not yet begun—for example, the state as a machine, the state as an organism, the king as the keystone of an arch, as a flag, or as the soul of a ship—the imagery of balance is most important for the modern age. Since the sixteenth century the image of a balance can be found in every aspect of intellectual life (Woodrow Wilson was certainly the first to acknowledge this in his speeches on freedom): a balance of trade in international economics, the European balance of power in foreign politics, the cosmic equilibrium of attraction and repulsion, the balance of the passions in the works of Malebranche and Shaftesbury, even a balanced diet is recommended by J. J. Moser. The importance for state theory of this universally employed conception is demonstrated by a few names: Harrington, Locke, Bolingbroke, Montesquieu, Mably, de Lolme, *The Federalist*, and the French National Assembly of 1789. To give just two modern examples: Maurice Hauriou, in his "Principes de droit public," applies the notion of equilibrium to every problem of the state and administration, and the enormous success of Robert Redslob's definition of parliamentary government (1918) demonstrates how powerful this theory is even today.[17]

Applied to the institution of parliament this general conception takes on a specific meaning. This has to be emphasized because it dominates even Rousseau's thought, although there it does not have this particular application to parliament.[18] Here, in parliament, there is a balance that assumes the moderate rationalism of this concept of the balance of powers. Under the suggestive influence of a compendium tradition, which Montesquieu's theory of the division of powers simplified,[19] one has become accustomed to seeing parliament as only a part of the state's functions, one part that is set against the others (executive and courts). Nevertheless, parliament should not be just a part of this balance, but precisely because it is the legislative, parliament should itself be balanced. This depends on a way of thinking that creates multiplicity everywhere so that an equilibrium created from the imminent dynamics of a system of negotiations replaces absolute unity. First through this processs can the legislative itself be balanced and mediated either in a bicameral system or through federalism; but even within a single chamber the balancing of outlooks and opinions functions as a consequence of this special kind of rationalism. An opposition belongs to the essence of parliament and every chamber, and there is actually a metaphysic of the two-party system. Normally a rather banal sentence is quoted, usually from Locke, to justify the balance of power theory.[20] It would be dangerous if the offices which make the laws were also to execute them; that would be too much temptation to the human desire for power. Therefore, neither the prince as head of the executive nor the parliament as legislative organ should be allowed to unite all state power in themselves. The first theories of the division and balance of power developed, after all, from an experience of the concentration of power in the Long Parliament of 1640.[21] But as soon as a justification in political theory was established, a constitutional theory with a constitutional concept of legislation appeared on the Continent. According to this, the institution of parliament must be understood as an essentially legislative state organ. Only this legislative concept justifies a notion that is scarcely understood today but which has held an absolutely dominant position in West European thought since the middle of the eighteenth century: that a constitution is identical with division of power. In article 16 of the Declaration of the Rights of Man and Citizens of 1789 can be found its most famous proclamation: "Any society in which the separation of powers and rights is not guaranteed has no constitution."[22] That the division of powers and a constitution are identical and that this defines the concept of a constitution even appears in German political thought from Kant to Hegel as a given. In consequence such a theory understands dictatorship not just as an antithesis of democracy but also essentially as the suspension of the division of powers, that is, as a suspension of the constitution, a suspension of the distinction between legislative and executive.[23]

3 The concept of law and legislation in parliamentarism

The parliamentary conception of legislation is already recognizable
with the Monarchomachians. In his *Droit des Magistrats*, Beza writes:
"One should not judge by cases, but by the law."[24] The *Vindiciae* of
Junius Brutus was directed against the "pernicious doctrine" of Machiavelli, and displays not only a passionate feeling of justice but also
a certain kind of rationalism. The author wanted to advance "mathematical ethics" and replace the concrete person of the king with an
impersonal *authority* and a universal *reason*, which according to Aris-
totelian-scholastic tradition constitutes the essence of law. The king
must obey the law as the body obeys the soul. The universal criterion
of the law is deduced from the fact that law (in contrast to will or the
command of a concrete person) is only *reason*, not desire, and that it
has no *passions*, whereas a concrete person "is moved by a variety of
particular passions."[25] In many different versions, but always with the
essential characteristic of the "universal," this concept of legislation
has become the foundation of constitutional theory. Grotius presents
it in the scholastic form of the universal in contrast to the particular.[26]
The whole theory of the *Rechtsstaat* rests on the contrast between law
which is general and already promulgated, universally binding without
exception, and valid in principle for all times, and a personal order
which varies case to case according to particular concrete circumstances.
In a well-known exposition, Otto Mayer talks about the inviolability
of the law.[27] This conception of law is based on a rationalistic distinction
between the (no longer universal but) general and the particular, and
representatives of *Rechtsstaat* thinking believe that the general has a
higher value, in itself, than the particular. This becomes especially
clear in the juxtaposition of law and commission, which belongs to
the center of Locke's argument. This classical theorist of the philosophy
of the *Rechtsstaat*[28] is only one example of the controversy that has
gone on for more than a century over the question of whether the
impersonal law or the king personally is sovereign.[29] Even "the gov-

ernment of the United States of America can be designated with particular emphasis as a government of laws in contrast to a government of men."[30] The usual definition of sovereignty today rests on Bodin's recognition that it will always be necessary to make exceptions to the general rule in concrete circumstances, and that the sovereign is whoever decides what constitutes an exception.[31] The cornerstone, therefore, of constitutional and absolutist thought is a concept of law. Not of course the concept that in Germany one has called law in the formal sense ever since Laband,[32] according to which everything that comes into existence with the agreement of the popular assembly can be called law, but rather a principle that accords with certain logical attributes. The crucial distinction always remains whether the law is a general rational principle or a measure, a concrete decree, an order.

If only those regulations which have come into effect with the cooperation and participation of the popular assembly are called laws, then it is because the popular assembly, that is, the parliament, has taken its decisions according to a parliamentary method, considering arguments and counterarguments. As a consequence its decisions have a logically different character from that of commands which are only based on authority. This is expressed in the biting antitheses of Hobbes's definition of law: "Every man seeth, that some lawes are addressed to all the subjects in generall, some to particular Provinces; some to particular Vocations; and some to particular Men." To an absolutist it is obvious "that Law is not Counsell, but Command,"[33] essentially authority and not, as in the rationalist conception of the law in *Rechtsstaat* theories, truth and justice: *Autoritas, non Veritas facit Legem* ("Authority, not truth, makes the law"). Bolingbroke, who as a representative of the balance of powers theory of government thought in terms of the *Rechtsstaat*, formulated the contrast as one of "Government by constitution" and "Government by will." He distinguished between constitution and government so that the constitution contained a system of rules that is always and *at all times* valid, whereas government was what actually occurred *at any time*; the one is unchanging, and the other changes with time and circumstances.[34] The theory of law as the General Will (a will that is valuable as such because of its general character, in contrast to every particular will), which dominated political thought throughout the seventeenth and eighteenth centuries, can be understood as an expression of the concept of law in a *Rechtsstaat*. Here, too, Condorcet is the typical representative of enlightened radicalism, for whom everything concrete is only a case for the application of a general law. Every activity, the whole life of the state, according to Condorcet, exhausts itself in law and the application of law; even the executive has only the function "of pronouncing a syllogism in which the law is the major premise; a more or less general fact is the minor premise; and the conclusion is the application of the law." Justice is not only, as Montesquieu said, "the mouth that pronounces the words of the law" but the administration as well.[35] In the design of the Girondist constitution of 1793 this principle was to be firmly established in the distinguishing characteristic of the law: "The characteristic that distinguishes the laws is to be found in their generality and unlimited duration."[36] Even the executive should no longer command, but only reason: "The agents of the executive do not command, they reason." The last example of the central, systematic distinction of law and command is offered in Hegel's argument about the legal character of a budget law: The so-called financial law is, despite the cooperation of the corporations, essentially a government prerogative. It is thus inappropriately called a law because it embraces the widest, even the complete, extent of government and the means of government. "A law passed each year for only a year will seem unreasonable even to the common man who distinguishes the substantial universality of a true law from that which is, by its nature, only superficially general."[37]

4 Parliament limited to legislation

Law, *Veritas* in contrast to mere *Autoritas*, the generally correct norm in contrast to the merely real and concrete order as Zitelmann argued in a brilliant formulation,[38] as an imperative always contains an individual nontransferable moment; this idea of law has always been conceived as something intellectual, unlike the executive, which is essentially active. Legislation is *deliberare*, executive *agere*. This contrast too has a history, one that begins with Aristotle. The rationalism of the French Enlightenment emphasized the legislative at the expense of the executive, and it found a potent formula for the executive in the constitution of 5 Fructidor III (Title IX, 275): "No armed force can deliberate."[39] The least doctrinaire explanation of this principle is to be found in *The Federalist* (1788): The executive must be in the hand of a single man because its energy and activity depend upon that; it is a general principle recognized by the best politicians and statesmen that legislation is deliberation and therefore must be made by a larger assembly, while decision making and protection of state secrets belong to the executive, things which "decline in the same measure as the numbers increase." A few historical examples are given for this, and the argument of *The Federalist* then goes on: Let us set aside the uncertainty and confusion of historical reflection and affirm what reason and sound judgment tell us; the guarantee of civic freedom can only be logically implemented in the legislative, not in the executive; in the legislative the opposition of opinions and parties may hinder many useful and correct decisions, but the arguments of the minority do contain or reduce the excesses of the majority in this way. Different opinions are useful and necessary in the legislative; but not in the executive, where especially in times of war and disturbance action must be energetic; to this belongs a unity of decision.[40]

This moderate argument in *The Federalist* shows most clearly how little consideration was given in the balance theory to extending the rationalism that is authoritative in the legislative branch and parliament to the executive as well and thus dissolving it, too, into discussion. The rationalism of this theory even maintains a balance between the rational and the irrational (if this is what one calls things that are not accessible through rational discussion), and even here there is negotiation and a certain compromise, just as deism can be conceived as a metaphysical compromise.[41] By contrast, Condorcet's absolute rationalism negates the division of powers and destroys both its inherent negotiation and moderation of state powers and the independence of the parties. To his radicalism, the complicated balancing of the American constitution appeared subtle and difficult, a concession to the peculiarities of that land, one of those systems "where one must enforce the laws and in consequence truth, reason and justice,"[42] and where one must sacrifice "rational legislation" to the prejudices and stupidity of individual people. Such rationalism led to the elimination of balance and to a rational dictatorship. Both the American constitution and Condorcet identify law with truth; but the relative rationalism of the balance theory was limited to the legislative and logically limited again within parliament to a merely relative truth. A balance of opinions achieved through the contradiction and opposition of the parties can as a consequence never extend to absolute questions of an ideology, but can only concern things that are by their nature relative and therefore appropriate for this purpose. Contradictory oppositions eliminate parliamentarism, and parliamentary discussion assumes a common, indisputable foundation. Neither state power nor any kind of metaphysical conviction is allowed to appear immediately within its sphere; everything must be negotiated in a deliberately complicated process of balancing. Parliament is the place where one deliberates, that is, where a relative truth is achieved through discourse, in the discussion of argument and counterargument. Just as a multiplicity of powers is necessary for the state, so every parliamentary body needs multiple parties.

In German liberalism during the first half of the nineteenth century, these ideas were already bound up with historical thought. Surely the balance theory, with its elasticity and mediating capacity, could also integrate historical thought into its system. It is of great interest how the mechanical conception of balance was developed within nineteenth-century German liberalism in a peculiar way into a theory of organic agency and thus always retained, too, the possibility of accepting the prince as a preeminent person representing the unity of the state. While liberal discussion became an eternal conversation in German romanticism,[43] in the philosophical system of Hegel it is the self-development of consciousness out of positions and negations into always new syntheses. Hegel limited the Estates to a purely advisory role, and understood the function of corporative representation as that of bringing into existence "the public consciousness as an empirical universal, of which the thoughts and opinions of the many are particulars." The Estates are a mediating organ between the government and the people, which have only an advisory role in legislation; through the openness of their deliberations "the moment of formal freedom shall come into its right in respect of those members of civil society who are without any share in the executive," and general knowledge shall be extended and increased. "Through the opening of this opportunity to know . . . public opinion first reaches thoughts that are true and attains an insight into the situation and concept of the state and its affairs, and so first acquires ability to estimate these more rationally." Hence this kind of parliamentarism is an educational means, "and indeed one of the greatest."[44] On the value of openness and public opinion Hegel delivers a characteristic comment: "Estates Assemblies, open to the public, are a great spectacle and an excellent education for the citizens, and it is from them that the people learns best how to recognize the true character of its interests." The vitality of state interests first comes into existence in this way. "Public opinion is," for Hegel, "the unorganized way in which a people's opinions and wishes are made known." The theory of parties in German liberalism also contains a conception of organic life. There a distinction is made between parties and factions, in which the latter are caricatures of parties, whereas true parties are the expression of "living and multiple aspects of the public being . . . concerned with the proper disposition of public or state questions through a vigorous struggle."[45] Bluntschli, who took over F. Rohmer's theory of parties, says that a party cannot exist without an opposite party, that only the prince and civil servants (and these as such, not as private persons) are prohibited from membership in a party, because the state and its organs exist above the parties. "Constitutional law does not recognize parties; the calm and settled organization of the state is the common, firm order for everything, and it limits party business and party struggle. . . . Only if the movement of a new free life starts when politics begins do the parties appear." The parties are for him (following Rohmer) analogous to various stages of life. One also finds here a conception that Lorenz von Stein developed in its classic form: that contradictions belong to the life of the state just as they do to individual lives, and that these constitute the dynamic of something really living.[46]

On this point liberal thought merges with a specifically German organic theory and overcomes the mechanical conception of balance. But one could still hold onto the idea of parliamentarism with the help of this organic theory. As soon as there is a demand for parliamentary government, such as Mohl's, the idea of parliamentarism finds itself in a crisis because the perspective of a dialectic-dynamic process of discussion can certainly be applied to the legislative but scarcely to the executive. Only a universally applicable law, not a concrete order, can unite truth and justice through the balance of negotiations and public discussion. The old conception of parliament remained secure in these conclusions even in particular points, without their systematic interdependence being made clear. Bluntschli, for example, set out as an essential characteristic of modern parliament that it should not conclude its business in committees as the old corporative assembly had done.[47] That is completely correct; but this conclusion is derived from principles of openness and discussion that were no longer current.

5 The general meaning of the belief in discussion

Openness and discussion are the two principles on which constitutional thought and parliamentarism depend in a thoroughly logical and comprehensive system. For the sense of justice of an entire historical epoch, they seemed to be essential and indispensable. What was to be secured through the balance guaranteed by openness and discussion was nothing less than truth and justice itself. One believed that naked power and force—for liberal, *Rechtsstaat* thinking, an evil in itself, "the way of beasts," as Locke said[48]—could be overcome through openness and discussion alone, and the victory of right over might achieved. There is an utterly typical expression for this way of thinking: "discussion in place of force." In this formulation, it comes from a man who was certainly not brilliant, not even important, but a typical adherent, perhaps, of the bourgeois monarchy. He summarized the warp and woof of the whole complex fabric of constitutional and parliamentary thought: All progress, including social progress, is realized "through representative institutions, that is, regulated liberty— through public discussion, that is, reason."[49]

The reality of parliamentary and party political life and public convictions are today far removed from such beliefs. Great political and economic decisions on which the fate of mankind rests no longer result today (if they ever did) from balancing opinions in public debate and counterdebate. Such decisions are no longer the outcome of parliamentary debate. The participation of popular representatives in government—parliamentary government—has proven the most effective means of abolishing the division of powers, and with it the old concept of parliamentarism. As things stand today, it is of course practically impossible not to work with committees, and increasingly smaller committees; in this way the parliamentary plenum gradually drifts away from its purpose (that is, from its public), and as a result it necessarily becomes a mere façade. It may be that there is no other practical alternative. But one must then at least have enough awareness of the historical situation to see that parliamentarism thus abandons its intellectual foundation and that the whole system of freedom of speech, assembly, and the press, of public meetings, parliamentary immunities and privileges, is losing its rationale. Small and exclusive committees of parties or of party coalitions make their decisions behind closed doors, and what representatives of the big capitalist interest groups agree to in the smallest committees is more important for the fate of millions of people, perhaps, than any political decision. The idea of modern parliamentarism, the demand for checks, and the belief in openness and publicity were born in the struggle against the secret politics of absolute princes. The popular sense of freedom and justice was outraged by arcane practices that decided the fate of nations in secret resolutions. But how harmless and idyllic are the objects of cabinet politics in the seventeenth and eighteenth centuries compared with the fate that is at stake today and which is the subject of all manner of secrets. In the face of this reality, the belief in a discussing public must suffer a terrible disillusionment. There are certainly not many people today who want to renounce the old liberal freedoms, particularly freedom of speech and the press. But on the European continent there are not many more who believe that these freedoms still exist where they could actually endanger the real holders of power. And the smallest number still believe that just laws and the right politics can be achieved through newspaper articles, speeches at demonstrations, and parliamentary debates. But that is the very belief in parliament. If in the actual circumstances of parliamentary business, openness and discussion have become an empty and trivial formality, then parliament, as it developed in the nineteenth century, has also lost its previous foundation and its meaning.

3

Dictatorship in Marxist Thought

Constitutional parliamentarism had its classical period on the European continent in the bourgeois monarchy of Louis-Philippe and its classical representative in Guizot. For it, the ancient monarchy and aristocracy were defeated, and the approach of democracy appeared a chaotic storm against which a dam had to built. The constitutional-parliamentary monarchy of the bourgeoisie hovered between these two, monarchy and democracy. All social questions were to be resolved by parliament in rational, open debate; the term *juste milieu* came from the innermost core of such thought, and a concept such as bourgeois monarchy already contains within itself a whole world of *juste milieu* and principled compromise. In opposition to parliamentary constitutionalism, not to democracy, the idea of a dictatorship that would sweep away parliamentarism regained its topicality. The critical year 1848 was a year of democracy and of dictatorship at the same time. Both stood in opposition to the bourgeois liberalism of parliamentary thought.[1]

Discussing, balancing, engaging in principled negotiations, this thought stood between two adversaries who opposed it with such energy that the very idea of mediating discussion appeared to be only an interim between bloody battles. Both opponents answered with a destruction of balance, with an immediacy and absolute certainty—with dictatorship. There is, to use crude catchwords for a provisional characterization, a dogma of rationalism and another of irrationalism. For the dictatorship born of an unmediated rationalism that is absolutely certain in its own terms, a long tradition already lay at hand: the Enlightenment's educational dictatorship, philosophical Jacobinism, the tyranny of reason, a formal unity springing from the rationalist and classical spirit, the "alliance of philosophy and the sword."[2] With Napoleon's defeat this tradition appeared to be finished, overcome theoretically and morally by a newly awakening historical sense. But the possibility of a rationalist dictatorship always remained in a historical-philosophical form and lived on as a political idea. Its upholder was radical Marxist socialism, whose ultimate metaphysical proof was built on the basis of Hegel's historical logic.

Just because socialism moved from utopia to science does not mean that it renounced dictatorship. It is a remarkable symptom that a few radical socialists and anarchists have believed since the World War that they must go back to a utopia so that socialism can regain its courage for dictatorship.[3] This demonstrates how profoundly science has ceased to be the obvious foundation of social practice for the current generation. But it does not prove that the possibility of a dictatorship is no longer open to scientific socialism. The word *scientific* must only be correctly understood, and not limited to merely precise natural-scientific technology. The philosophy of the natural sciences cannot, of course, provide a foundation for dictatorship just as it could not for any other political institution or authority. The rationalism of scientific socialism goes much further than the natural sciences could possibly do. In it the rationalist faith of the Enlightenment has been vastly outdone and taken a new, almost fantastic jump. Had it been able to retain its old energy, then it would certainly have been comparable in intensity with the rationalism of the Enlightenment.

1 Marxist science is metaphysics

Only when it was scientifically formulated did socialism believe itself in possession of an essentially infallible truth, and just at that moment it claimed the right to use force. The scientific certainty of socialism appeared historically after 1848, that is, after socialism had become a political power that could hope to realize its ideas one day. In this kind of science practical and theoretical conceptions mingle. Very often scientific socialism meant only a negative, the rejection of utopia and the determination from then on to intervene consciously in social and political reality. Instead of being conceived from the outside according to fantasies and splendid ideals, social and political reality was to be analyzed from within, according to its actual and correctly understood immanent circumstances. Here it is a matter of looking for the ultimate and, in an intellectual sense, decisive argument among the many sides and possibilities of socialism for the final evidence of socialist belief. Convinced Marxism holds that it has found the true explanation for social, economic, and political life, and that a correct praxis follows from that knowledge; it follows that social life can be correctly grasped immanently in all of its objective necessity and thus controlled. Because Marx and Engels, and certainly every Marxist capable of intellectual fanaticism, have a lively awareness of the contingencies of historical development, one cannot compare their science to the many attempts that have been made to apply the methods of natural science and exactitude to the problems of social philosophy and politics. Of course vulgar Marxism is glad to claim a natural-scientific exactness for its theory and the "iron necessity" produced by the laws of historical materialism. Many bourgeois social philosophers have concerned themselves with the attempt to refute that claim and prove that one cannot deal with historical events in the same way that astronomy can calculate the movements of the stars and that in any case—even admitting an "iron necessity"—it would be peculiar to organize a political party for the achievement of a coming eclipse of the sun. But the rationalism of Marxist theory has another side, more important for the concept of dictatorship. This rationalism does not exhaust itself in a science that intends, with the help of natural laws and strict determinism, to produce a method that would be used to turn the laws of nature to mankind's advantage, as, for example, a technique is bound to an exact natural-scientific method. If that were the scientific in socialism, then the leap into the realm of freedom would only be a leap into the realm of absolute technocracy. It would have been only a remnant of an earlier Enlightenment rationalism and another example of the attempt, much favored since the eighteenth century,[4] to produce a politics of mathematical and physical exactness, with the sole difference that the powerful moralism that still dominated eighteenth-century thought would be given up theoretically. The result must be, as with all rationalisms, a dictatorship of the leading rationalists.

The philosophically and metaphysically fascinating aspect of Marxist historical philosophy and sociology is not its similarity to natural science, but the way that Marx retains the concept of a dialectical development of human history and observes this development as a concrete, unique antithetical process, producing itself through an immanent, organic power. It changes nothing in the structure of his thought that he shifted this development into the area of economics and technology. This is merely a transference that can be explained in various ways: for example, psychologically, from an intuition about the political importance of economic factors, or systematically, from the attempt to make human activity the master of historical events, the master of the irrationality of human fate. The "leap into the realm of freedom" can only be understood dialectically. It cannot be undertaken with the help of technique alone. Otherwise one could really demand of Marxist socialism that instead of political action, it would do better to invent new machines. It might be conceivable that in the future communist society, new technical and chemical discoveries might be made which would again alter the foundations of communist society and make a revolution necessary. Finally, it is peculiar to assume, for once and for all, that this future society must give tremendous support to technical development, accelerating its tempo, and on the other hand be constantly protected from the danger that a new organization of classes would pose. All these objections are quite plausible, but they do not touch the heart of this theory. According to Marxist belief, humanity will become conscious of itself and that will occur precisely by means of the correct knowledge of social reality. Consciousness thus achieves an absolute character. Here it is a matter of a rationalism that includes Hegelian evolution within itself and finds its proof in its own concreteness, something of which the abstract rationalism of the Enlightenment was not capable. Marxist science does not want to attribute to coming events the mechanical certainty of a mechanically calculated and mechanically constructed triumph; rather, this is left to the flow of time and the concrete reality of historical events, which are producing themselves from out of themselves.

Marx always knew that an understanding of concrete historicity was an advantage. But Hegel's rationalism had the courage to construct history itself. An active person then could have no other interest than to grasp with absolute certainty current events and the contemporary epoch. That was scientifically possible with the help of a dialectical construction of history. The science of Marxist socialism rests, therefore, on the principle of the Hegelian philosophy of history. This is to show not that Marx is dependent upon Hegel and thus to increase the numerous analyses of their relationship, but rather that in order to define the core of Marx's argument and its specific concept of dictatorship, one must begin with the connection between Hegel's historical dialectic and Marx's political theory. It will be shown that there is a peculiar kind of metaphysical evidence here that leads to certain sociological constructions and to a rationalist dictatorship.

2 Dictatorship and dialectical development

It is indeed difficult to connect dialectical development and dictatorship, because dictatorship seems to be an interruption of the continual series of development, a mechanical intervention in organic evolution. Development and dictatorship seem to be mutually exclusive. The unending process of a world spirit that develops itself in contradictions must also include within itself even its own real contradiction, dictatorship, and thus rob it of its essence, decision. Development goes on without a break and even interruptions must serve it as negations so that it wil be pushed further. The essential point is that an exception never comes from outside into the immanence of development. Hegel's philosophy, in any case, was not concerned with dictatorship in the sense of a moral decision that interrupts the process of development or discussion. Even the most contradictory things assert themselves and will be incorporated in an encompassing development. The either/or of moral decision, the decisive and deciding disjunction, has no place in this system. Even the *diktat* of a dictator becomes a moment in the discussion and in the undisturbed development as it moves further. Just as everything else, the *diktat* too will be assimilated by the peristalsis of the world spirit. Hegel's philosophy contains no ethic that could provide a foundation for the absolute distinction of good and evil. According to this philosophy, the good is what is rational at the current station of the dialectical process and thereby what is real. Good is (I accept here Christian Janentzky's pertinent formulation) "the current," in the sense of being a correct dialectical knowledge and consciousness. If world history is also the world court,[5] then it is a process without a last instance and without a definitive, disjunctive judgment. Evil is unreal and only conceivable insofar as something out-of-date can be thought, and thus perhaps explicable as a false abstraction of reason, a passing confusion of a particularity closed in upon itself.

Only within an at least theoretically small area—to overcome what is out-of-date or to correct false appearances—would a dictatorship be possible. It would be something peripheral and incidental, not the essential negation of the essential, but the removal of an inconsequential bit of rubbish. In contrast to Fichte's rationalist philosophy, here a despotism is rejected. Against Fichte, Hegel argued that it would be a violent abstraction to assume that the world had been abandoned by God and was only waiting until mankind could bring a purpose to it and build it according to an abstract notion of "how things should be."[6] An "ought" is impotent. What is right will make itself effective, and what merely should be, without actually existing, is not true but only a subjective mastery of life.

The most important advance that the nineteenth century made over the rationalism of the eighteenth rests on this contrast between Hegel and Fichte. A dictatorship had become impossible because the absolute character of moral disjunction had been dissolved. Nevertheless Hegel's philosophy remained only a logical development and intensification of the old rationalism. The conscious human act first makes people what they are and propels them out of the natural finitude of an "in-itself" onto the higher level of a "for-itself." What man is according to his aptitude and ability he must first become aware of, so that he does not remain trapped in a merely accidental and capricious empirical existence and so that the irresistible motion of world-historical events do not pass him by. So long as this philosophy remained contemplative, it had no place for dictatorship in any case. But that changes as soon as it is taken seriously by active people. In material political and sociological praxis, those who have a higher consciousness and who believe themselves to be representatives of this great force will shake off the constraints of a narrow outlook, and will enforce the "objectively necessary." Here too their will forces the unfree to be free. In practice that is an educational dictatorship. But if world history is to go forward, if the unreal must be continually defeated, then by necessity the dictatorship will become permanent. Here it is also clear that the universal duality, which, according to Hegel's philosophy, can be found in everything that happens, rests above all in itself: Its concept of development can eliminate dictatorship just as it could declare a permanent dictatorship. For the actions of people, there is always the argument that the highest level of consciousness can and must exercise dominion over the lower. In political and practical terms that is the equivalent of a rationalist educational dictator. But Hegelianism, like every rationalist system, thus negates the individual as accidental and inessential, and elevates the whole systematically into an absolute.

The *Weltgeist* only manifests itself in a few minds at any stage of its development. The spirit of an age does not thrust itself into the awareness of every person at a single stroke, nor does it appear in all members of the dominant nation or social group. There will always be a vanguard of the *Weltgeist*, the apex of the development of consciousness, an avant-garde that has the right to act because it possesses correct knowledge and consciousness, not as the chosen of a personal God, but as a moment in development. This vanguard does not wish to escape from the immanence of world-historical evolution at all, but is, according to the vulgar image, the midwife of coming things. The world-historical personality—Theseus, Caesar, Napoleon—is an instrument of the *Weltgeist*; his *diktat* rests upon his position in the historical moment. The world soul that Hegel saw riding by in Jena in 1806 was a soldier, not a Hegelian.[7] It was the representative of the alliance between philosophy and the saber but only from the side of the saber. But it was Hegelians, conscious of knowing their own time correctly, who demanded a political dictatorship in which they naturally would become the dictators. In no way different from Fichte, they were "ready to prove to the world that their view was infallible." That gave them the right to dictatorship.[8]

3 Dictatorship and dialectics in Marxist socialism

The interpretation of Hegel's philosophy presented here, that it has a side whose practical consequences can lead to a rationalist dictatorship, also holds true for Marxism, and certainly in the kind of proof on which the metaphysical certainty of dictatorship is founded it has remained completely within the sphere of Hegelian historical constructions. Because Marx's scientific interests later developed almost exclusively into national economic interests (that was also, as will momentarily be shown, a consequence of Hegelian thought) and because the decisive concept of class had not yet been worked into the philosophy of history and a sociological system, a superficial observation can shift the essence of Marxism onto the materialist theory of history. But the real historical construction already appears in *The Communist Manifesto*, whose lines have always remained fundamental. That world history is the history of class struggle had already been known for a long time; *The Communist Manifesto* offers nothing really new in this respect. And by 1848 the bourgeois was already long familiar as a figure of spite; scarcely any significant literature of that time did not use the word as a term of abuse.[9] What was new and fascinating in *The Communist Manifesto* was something else: The systematic concentration of class struggle into a single, final struggle of human history, into the dialectical peak of tension between bourgeoisie and proletariat. The contradictions of many classes were thus simplified into a single, final contradiction. In place of many earlier classes, even in place of the three classes identified by Ricardo (capitalists, landowners, and wage workers) and accepted by Marx in the details of political economy in *Capital*,[10] there appears a single class contradiction. This simplification signified a powerful increase in intensity. It asserted itself with systematic and methodical necessity. Because the process of development is dialectical and therefore logical, even if its basis remains economics, a simple antithesis must emerge in the last critical, absolutely decisive turning point of world history. In this way the greatest tension of the world-historical moment arises. On this logical simplification rests the final intensification not only of real struggle but also of theoretical contradictions. Everything must be forced to the extreme so that it can be overturned out of dialectical necessity. The most monstrous wealth must confront the most horrific misery; the class that owns everything must face the class that owns nothing; the bourgeois, who only possesses, who only has and who is no longer human, opposes the proletarian, who has nothing and who is nothing but a person. Without the dialectics of Hegel's philosophy it is completely unimaginable that, on the basis of all previous experience of history, this process of pauperization has gone on for centuries and that mankind would finally either sink under the weight of universal oppression or a new mass migration would change the face of the earth. The communist society of the future, the higher stage of a classless humanity, is thus only evident when socialism retains the structure of Hegelian dialectics. Then the inhumanity of the capitalist social order must of necessity produce its own negation from within itself.

Under the influence of this dialectic, Lassalle had also tried to push this tension to antithetical extremes, even if he was more motivated by rhetorical than by theoretical interests when he replied to Schulze-Delitsch: "Ricardo is the greatest theorist of the bourgeois economy. He led it to its summit, to a precipice where the only theoretical development left to it was its transformation into social economy."[11] The bourgeoisie must therefore reach its most extreme intensification before it appears certain that its last hour has come. Lassalle and Marx are in complete agreement about this essential conception. The simplification of contradictions into a final, absolute class conflict first brings about the critical moment of the dialectical process. But still, where does the certainty come from that the moment has arrived, and that this is the last hour of the bourgeoisie? If one examines the kind of evidence Marxists use to argue this point, a tautology that is typical for Hegelian rationalism will be immediately recognizable. The construction starts from the assumption that the evolution of a constantly increasing consciousness means—and its own certainty of this consciousness is offered as evidence for it—that it is correct. The dialectical construction of increasing consciousness forces the constructing thinker to think himself with his thought as the peak of this development. For him that means at the same time the attainment of his own perfect knowledge of the phases of the historical past which lay behind him. He would not think correctly and would contradict himself if this development were not most deeply conscious of itself in his thought. If an epoch can be grasped in human consciousness, then that furnishes proof for a historical dialectic that this epoch is historically finished. For the face of the thinker is turned toward the historical, that is, toward the past and the passing present; nothing is more false than the popular belief that Hegelians believed they could foresee the future like a prophet. The thinker, however, only knows coming things concretely in the negative, as the dialectical contradiction of what is already historically finished. He discovers the past as a development into the present, which he sees in its continuous evolution; and if he has correctly understood it and correctly constructed it, then there is the certainty that this, as a thing known perfectly, belongs to the consciousness of a stage that has already been overcome and whose last hour has arrived.

In spite of expressions such as *iron necessity*, Marx did not calculate coming things as an astronomer calculates coming constellations of the stars; in the same way he was not what psychologial journalism tries to make of him, a Jewish prophet who prophesied future catastrophe. That Marx has a powerful moral pathos that influences his argument and descriptions is not difficult to recognize, but it is not specific to Marx any more than is a venomous contempt for the bourgeoisie. Both can be found in many nonsocialists as well. Marx's achievement was to lift the bourgeois out of the sphere of aristocratic and literary resentment and elevate him into a world-historical figure who must be absolutely inhuman, not in a moral sense, but in the Hegelian sense, in order to appeal from an immediate necessity to the good and absolutely human as its contradiction, just as Hegel argues that "it can be said of the Jewish people that precisely because they stand directly before the gates of heaven that they are the most profligate."[12] In Marxist terms it can only be said of the proletariat that it will be the absolute negation of the bourgeoisie. It would be an unscientific socialism if a description of the proletarian state of the future were to be painted into this picture. It is a systematic necessity that everything affecting the proletariat only allows itself to be negatively determined. Only when one had completely forgotten that could one attempt to determine the proletariat positively. Accordingly all that can be said about this future society is that it will have no class contradictions, and the proletariat can only be defined as the social class that no longer participates in profit, that owns nothing, that knows no ties to family or fatherland, and so forth. The proletarian becomes the social nonentity.[13] It must also be true that the proletarian, in contrast to the bourgeois, is nothing but a person. From this it follows with dialectic necessity that in the period of transition he can be nothing but a member of his class; that is, he must realize himself precisely in something that is the contradiction of humanity—in the class. The class contradiction must become the absolute contradiction so that all contradictions can be absolutely overcome and disappear into pure humanity.

4 The Marxist tautology

The scientific certainty of Marxism, therefore, only relates to the proletariat negatively conceived, insofar as it is economically the dialectical contradiction of the bourgeoisie. In contrast, the bourgeoisie must be known positively and in its full historicity. Because its essence lies in the economic, Marx has to follow it into the economic realm in order to understand it fully and in its essence. If he could succeed, if he could know the bourgeoisie absolutely, then that would prove that the bourgeoisie belonged to history, that it was finished, that it represented a stage of development the spirit had consciously overcome. For the scientific claim of Marxist socialism it is really a question of life and death, whether it is possible to analyze the bourgeoisie correctly and to grasp it intellectually. Here is the deepest motive for the demoniac assiduity with which Marx delved into economic questions. It has already been objected against him that while he hoped to discover the natural laws of economic and social life, his researches were limited almost exclusively to the industrial conditions of England as "the classical site" of the capitalist mode of production.[14] Moreover, his discussion remains limited to goods and values, and therefore to the concepts of bourgeois capitalism; thus he remained trapped in classical, and therefore bourgeois, political economy. Such accusations would be correct if the specifically scientific character of Marxism were to rest exclusively on sharp analysis. But science here means the consciousness of an evolutionary metaphysics that makes consciousness into the criterion of progress. The fantastic urgency with which Marx returns again and again to the bourgeois economy is therefore neither an academic-theoretical fanaticism nor simply a technical-tactical interest in his opponent. This insistence derives from a thoroughly metaphysical compulsion. A correct consciousness is the criterion for the beginning of a new stage of development. So long as this is not the case, so long as a new epoch is not really at hand, then the previous epoch (that is, the bourgeois epoch) cannot be correctly known, and vice versa: That the bourgeoisie *is* correctly understood again provides the evidence that its era is at an end. The tautology of Hegelian as well as of Marxist certainty moves in such circles, and provides a "self-guarantee' of its own truth. The scientific certainty that the historical moment of the proletariat has arrived is first produced, therefore, by a correct understanding of the process of development. The bourgeoisie cannot grasp the proletariat, but the proletariat can certainly grasp the bourgeoisie. With this the sun begins to set on the age of the bourgeoisie; the owl of Minerva begins its flight. But here that does not mean that the arts and sciences have progressed, but rather that the passing age has become an object of the historical consciousness of a new epoch.

Perhaps in its final state a Marxist humanity, one that has come into its own, will not be distinguishable from the final goal envisaged by the rationalist educational dictator for mankind. We need not follow this speculation any further. The rationalism that also incorporated world history into its construction certainly has its great dramatic moments; but its intensity ends in a fever, and it no longers sees the idyllic paradise before its eyes which the naive optimism of the Enlightenment saw and which Condorcet saw in his sketch of the development of the human race, in the "Apocalypse of the Enlightenment."[15] The new rationalism destroys itself dialectically, and before it stands a terrible negation. The kind of force to which it must resort cannot any longer be Fichte's naive schoolmasterly "educational dictatorship." The bourgeois is not to be educated, but eliminated. The struggle, a real and bloody struggle that arises here, requires a different chain of thought and a different intellectual constitution from the Hegelian construction, whose core always remained contemplative. The Hegelian construction remains the most important intellectual factor here, and almost every work by Lenin or Trotsky demonstrates how much energy and tension it can still generate. But it has become only an intellectual instrument for what is really no longer a rationalist impulse. The parties to the struggle that has broken out between the bourgeoisie and the proletariat had to assume a concrete shape, just as an actual struggle demands. A philosophy of material life offered an intellectual weapon for this purpose, a theory that saw every intellectual discovery as secondary compared to a deeper—more vital, emotional, or voluntary—course of events and that corresponded to a frame of mind in which the categories of received morals—the governance of the unconscious by the conscious, of instinct by reason— had been shaken to their very core. A new theory of the direct use of force arose in opposition to the absolute rationalsm of an educational dictatorship and to the relative rationalism of the division of powers. Against the belief in discussion there appeared a theory of direct action. Not only were the foundations of parliamentarism attacked, but so too the democracy that always remained, at least in theory, part of rationalist dictatorship. As Trotsky justly reminded the democrat Kautsky, the awareness of relative truths never gives one the courage to use force and to spill blood.[16]

4

Irrationalist Theories of the Direct Use of Force

It should be reiterated here that this examination directs its interest consistently toward the ideal circumstances of political and state philosophical tendencies, in order to understand the moral predicament of contemporary parliamentarism and the strength of the parliamentary idea. Even if the Marxist dictatorship of the proletariat still retains the possibility of the rationalist dictatorship, all modern theories of direct action and the use of force rest more or less consciously on an irrationalist philosophy. In reality, as happened in the Bolshevist regime, it appears that in political life many different movements and tendencies can be at work alongside each other. Although the Bolshevist government repressed the anarchists for political reasons, the complex to which the Bolshevist argument actually belongs contains an explicitly anarcho-syndicalist chain of thought. The Bolshevists' use of their political power to destroy the anarchists eradicates their shared intellectual history just as little as the repression of the Levellers by Cromwell destroyed his connection to them.[1] Perhaps Marxism has arisen so unrestrainedly on Russian soil because proletarian thought there had been utterly free of all the constrictions of Western European tradition and from all the moral and educational notions with which Marx and Engels themselves still quite obviously lived. The theory of a dictatorship of the proletariat, which is today officially accepted by the Marxist parties, would certainly be a good example of the fact that a rationalism conscious of its own historical development clamors for the use of force; and numerous parallels between the Jacobin dictatorship of 1793 and the Soviet system can be pointed to in the attitudes, in the arguments, in organizational and administrative application. The entire organization of teaching and education created by the Soviet government for its so-called *Proletkult* is an excellent example of a radical educational dictatorship.[2] But that does not explain why the idea of the industrial proletariat in the modern great city should have achieved such dominance precisely in Russia. The explanation can be found in the presence of a new irrationalist motive for the use of force that was also active there: This is not a rationalism that transforms itself through a radical exaggeration into its own opposite and fantasizes utopias, but finally a new evaluation of rational thought, a new belief in instinct and intuition that lays to rest every belief in discussion and would also reject the possibility that mankind could be made ready for discussion through an educational dictatorship.

Of those writings which are of interest here, only Enrico Ferri's "revolutionary method" is known in Germany, thanks to its translation by Robert Michels (in Grünberger's collection of the principal works of socialism).[3] The following exposition is based on Georges Sorel's *Réflexions sur la violence*, which allows the historical connection between these ideas to be recognized most clearly.[4] This book has in addition the advantage of many original historical and philosophical perceptions and acknowledges openly its intellectual debt to Proudhon, Bakunin, and Bergson. Its influence is noticeably greater than one can grasp at first glance, and it is certainly not refuted by the fact that Bergson has become passé.[5] Benedetto Croce believes that Sorel has given the Marxist dream a new form, but that the idea of democracy has triumphed among the working classes once and for all.[6] After the events and experiences in Russia and in Italy, one cannot any longer take that quite so much for granted. The foundation for Sorel's reflections on the use of force is a theory of unmediated real life, which was taken over from Bergson and, under the influence of two anarchists, Proudhon and Bakunin, applied to the problems of social life.

For Proudhon and Bakunin, anarchism meant a battle against every sort of systematic unity, against the centralized uniformity of the modern state, against the professional parliamentary politician, against bureaucracy, the military, and police, against what was felt to be the metaphysical centralism of belief in God. The analogy of both conceptions of God and the state forced themselves on Proudhon under the influence of restoration philosophy. He gave this philosophy a revolutionary antistate and antitheological twist, which Bakunin drew out to its logical conclusion.[7] The concrete individual, the social reality of life, is violently forced into an all-embracing system. The centralizing fanaticism of the Enlightenment is no less despotic than the unity and identity of modern democracy. Unity is slavery; all tyrannical institutions rest on centralism and authority, whether they are, as in modern democracy, sanctioned by universal suffrage or not.[8] Bakunin gave this struggle against God and the state the character of a struggle against intellectualism and against traditional forms of education altogether. With good reason he sees a new authority in the reliance on reason, a pretension to be the chief, the head, the mind of a movement. Even science does not have the right to rule. It is not life, it creates nothing, it constructs and receives, but it understands only the general and the abstract and sacrifices the individual fullness of life on the altar of its abstraction. Art is more important for the life of mankind than science. Such declarations by Bakunin are surprisingly in agreement with the thought of Bergson and they have rightly been emphasized.[9] From the unmediated immanent life of the working class itself one knows the importance of trade unions and their specific means of struggle, the strike. Thus Proudhon and Bakunin became the fathers of syndicalism and created that tradition on which, sup-

Irrationalist Theories of the Direct Use of Force

ported by arguments from Bergson's philosophy, Sorel's ideas are based. Its center is a theory of myth that poses the starkest contradiction of absolute rationalism and its dictatorship, but at the same time because it is a theory of direct, active decision, it is an even more powerful contradiction to the relative rationalism of the whole complex that is grouped around conceptions such as "balancing," "public discussion," and "parliamentarism."

The ability to act and the capacity for heroism, all world-historical activities reside, according to Sorel, in the power of myth. Examples of such myths are the Greeks' conception of fame and of a great name, the expectation of the Last Judgment in ancient Christianity, the belief in 'vertu' and in revolutionary freedom during the French Revolution, and the national enthusiasm of the German war of liberation in 1813. Only in myth can the criterion be found for deciding whether one nation or a social group has a historical mission and has reached its historical moment. Out of the depths of a genuine life instinct, not out of reason or pragmatism, springs the great enthusiasm, the great moral decision and the great myth. In direct intuition the enthusiastic mass creates a mythical image that pushes its energy forward and gives it the strength for martyrdom as well as the courage to use force. Only in this way can a people or a class become the engine of world history. Wherever this is lacking, no social and political power can remain standing, and no mechanical apparatus can build a dam if a new storm of historical life has broken loose. Accordingly, it is all a matter of seeing correctly where this capacity for myth and this vital strength are really alive today. In the modern bourgeoisie, which has collapsed into anxiety about money and property, in this social class morally ruined by skepticism, relativism, and parliamentarism, it is not to be found. The governmental form characteristic of this class, liberal democracy, is only a "demagogic plutocracy."[10] Who, then, is the vehicle of great myth today? Sorel attempted to prove that only the socialist masses of the industrial proletariat had a myth in which they believe, and this was the general strike. What the general strike really means today is much less important than the faith that binds the proletariat to it, the acts and sacrifices it inspires, and whether it might be able to produce a new morality. The belief that the general strike and the monstrous catastrophe it would provoke would subvert the whole of social and economic life thus belongs to the life of socialism. It has arisen out of the masses, out of the immediacy of the life of the industrial proletariat, not as a construction of intellectuals and literati, not as a utopia; for even utopia, according to Sorel, is the product of a rationalist intellect that attempts to conquer life from the outside, with a mechanistic scheme.

From the perspective of this philosophy, the bourgeois ideal of peaceful agreement, an ongoing and prosperous business that has advantages for everyone, becomes the monstrosity of cowardly intellectualism. Discussing, bargaining, parliamentary proceedings, appear a betrayal of myth and the enormous enthusiasm on which everything depends. Against the mercantilist image of balance there appears another vision, the warlike image of a bloody, definitive, destructive, decisive battle. In 1848 this image rose up on both sides in opposition to parliamentary constitutionalism: from the side of tradition in a conservative sense, represented by a Catholic Spaniard, Donoso-Cortés, and in radical anarcho-syndicalism in Proudhon. Both demanded a decision. All the Spaniard's thoughts were focused on the great battle (*la gran contienda*), the terrible catastrophe that lay ahead, which only the metaphysical cowardice of discursive liberalism could deny was coming. And Proudhon, for whose thought here the text *La Guerre et la paix* is characteristic, spoke of a Napoleonic battle, the "Bataille Napoléonienne," in which the enemy would be utterly annihilated.[11] All the brutality and violation of rights that belongs to a bloody struggle receives its historical sanction from Proudhon. Instead of relative oppositions accessible to parliamentary means, absolute antitheses now appear. "The day of radical rejection and the day of sovereign declarations is coming."[12] No parliamentary discussion can delay it; the people, driven forward by its instincts, will smash the pulpits of the sophists—all of these are opinions of Donoso-Cortés, which might have come word for word from Sorel, except that the anarchist stood on the side of the people's instinct. For Donoso-Cortés radical socialism was something enormous, greater than liberal moderation, because it went back to ultimate problems and gave a decisive answer to radical questions—because it had a theology. The opponent here was precisely Proudhon, not because he was the best-known socialist in 1848, against whom Montalembert had delivered a famous parliamentary speech,[13] but because he was a radical representative of radical principle. The Spaniard was dismayed in the face of the stupidity of the legitimists and the cowardly slyness of the bourgeoisie. Only in socialism did he still see what he called instinct (*el instinto*), and from that he concluded that in the long run all the parties were working for socialism. Thus the contradictions again assumed intellectual dimensions and often an obviously eschatological tension. In contrast to the dialectically constructed tensions of Hegelian Marxism, here it was a matter of the direct, intuitive contradiction of mythic images. Marx could regard Proudhon from the peak of his Hegelian education as a philosophical dilettante and show him how grossly he had misunderstood Hegel.[14] Today a radical socialist would be able to show Marx, with the help of a contemporary modern philosophy, that he was only a schoolmaster and remained trapped in an intellectual exaggeration of West European bourgeois education, whereas the poor, reprimanded Proudhon at least had an instinct for the real life of the working masses. In the eyes of Donoso-Cortés, this socialist anarchist was an evil demon, a devil, and for Proudhon the Catholic was a fanatical Grand Inquisitor, whom he attempted to laugh off. Today it is easy to see that both were their own real opponents and that everything else was only a provisional half-measure.[15]

The warlike and heroic conceptions that are bound up with battle and struggle were taken seriously again by Sorel as the true impulse of an intensive life. The proletariat must believe in the class struggle as a real battle, not as a slogan for parliamentary speeches and democratic electoral campaigns. It must grasp this struggle as a life instinct, without academic construction, and as the creator of a powerful myth in which it alone would find the courage for a decisive battle. For socialism and its ideas of class struggle there is no greater danger than professional politics and participation in parliamentary business. These wear down great enthusiasm into chatter and intrigue and kill the genuine instincts and intuitions that produce a moral decision. Whatever value human life has does not come from reason; it emerges from a state of war between those who are inspired by great mythical images to join battle, and depends upon "a state of war that the people agree to participate in, which is reflected in a certain myth."[16] Bellicose, revolutionary excitement and the expectation of monstrous catastrophes belong to the intensity of life and move history. But the momentum must come from the masses themselves; ideologists and intellectuals cannot create it. So the revolutionary wars of 1792 originated, as well as the epoch that Sorel along with Renan celebrated as the greatest peak of the nineteenth century, namely, the German war of liberation of 1813:[17] Its heroic spirit was born of the irrational life energy of an anonymous mass.

Every rationalist interpretation falsifies the immediacy of life. The myth is no utopia. For this, a product of rational thought leads at best to reforms. Nor should one confuse a martial élan with militarism; above all the use of force in this irrationalist philosophy was to be something other than a dictatorship. Sorel hated all intellectualism, all centralization, all uniformity, as did Proudhon, but he demanded nevertheless, like Proudhon, the strictest discipline and morale. The great battle will not be the work of an academic strategy, but an "accumulation of heroic exploits" and a release of the "individualistic forces within the rebelling mass."[18] Creative force that breaks loose in the spontaneity of enthusiastic masses is as a result something very different from dictatorship. Rationalism and all monisms that follow from it, like centralization and uniformity and even the bourgeois illusion of a "great man," belong to dictatorship, according to Sorel.

Their practical result is systematic subjugation and slavery, horror in the shape of justice and a mechanistic apparatus. Dictatorship is nothing but a military-bureaucratic-police machine, born from the rationalist spirit. In contrast, the revolutionary use of force by the masses is an expression of immediate life, often wild and barbaric, but never systematically horrible and inhuman.

The dictatorship of the proletariat also meant for Sorel, as for those who see it in the context of intellectual history, a repetition of 1793. When the revisionist Bernstein expressed the opinion that this dictatorship would probably be that of a club of talkers and literati, he certainly had in mind the imitation of 1793. Sorel answered him: The concept of a dictatorship of the proletariat is the received inheritance of the *ancien régime*.[19] It had the consequence that a new bureaucratic and military apparatus had to be set up in place of the old one, as the Jacobins had done. It would be a new regime of intellectuals and ideologists, but not proletarian freedom. Even Engels, from whom the phrase stems and who thought that a dictatorship of the proletariat would end as in 1793, was in Sorel's eyes a typical rationalist.[20] But it does not follow from this that the proletarian revolution must happen as a revisionist-pacifist-parliamentarian revolution. Rather in the place of the mechanically concentrated power of the bourgeois state there appears a creative proletarian force—"violence" appears in place of power. This is only a belligerent act, not a juridical and administrative measure. Marx did not yet know the difference, because he still lived with traditional political conceptions. The proletarian, unpolitical syndicates and the proletarian general strike have created specifically new means of struggle, which make the simple repetition of old political and military tactics completely impossible. For the proletariat, the only danger is that it might lose its weapons through parliamentary democracy and allow itself to be paralyzed.[21]

If one may reply to an irrationalist theory as decisive as this one with argument,[22] one must point out its numerous discrepancies—not its logical mistakes, but its inorganic contradictions. Above all

Sorel sought to retain the purely economic basis of the proletarian standpoint, and despite some disagreements, he clearly always began with Marx. He hoped that the proletariat would create a morality of economic producers. The class struggle is a struggle that takes place in the economic sphere with economic means. In the previous chapter it has been shown that Marx followed his opponent, the bourgeois, into economic territory out of systematic and logical necessity. Here, therefore, the enemy had determined the terrain on which one had to fight and also the weapons, that is, the structure of argumentation. If one followed the bourgeois into economic terrain, then one must also follow him into democracy and parliamentarism. Moreover, without the economic-technical rationalism of the bourgeois economy, then at least in the short term one would not be able to move about within the economic sphere. The mechanism of production created by the capitalist period has a rationalist regularity, and one can certainly create the courage to destroy it from a myth. But should this economic order develop even further, should production intensify even more, which Sorel obviously also wants, then the proletariat must renounce its myth. Just like the bourgeois, it will be forced, through the superior power of the production mechanism, into a rationalism and mechanistic outlook that is empty of myth. Marx was also here in an important sense more consequential because he was more rationalist. But looked at from the irrational, it was a betrayal to be even more economic and more rationalist than the bourgeoisie. Bakunin understood that completely. Marx's education and way of thinking remained traditional, bound down by what was then bourgeois, so that he always remained intellectually dependent on his opponent. In spite of that, it was exactly in Marx's construction of the bourgeois that his work was indispensable to Sorel's understanding of myth.

The great psychological and historical meaning of the social theory of myth cannot be denied. And the construction of the bourgeois by means of Hegelian dialectic has served to create an image of the enemy that was capable of intensifying all the emotions of hatred and contempt. I believe that the history of this image of the bourgeois is just as important as the history of the bourgeoisie itself. A figure of contempt first created by the aristocracy was propagated in the nineteenth century by romantic artists and poets. Since the growth of Stendhal's influence, all literati hold the bourgeoisie in contempt, even when they live off him or when they are the favorite lecturers of a bourgeois public, just as Murger with his *Bohème*. More important than such caricatures is the hatred of a socially déclassé genius such as Baudelaire, who infuses a new life into this image. The figure created in France by French authors based on the French bourgeois has taken on the dimension of a world-historical construction through the work of Marx and Engels. They gave it the meaning of the last representative of a prehistorical humanity that was divided into classes, the very last enemy of mankind, the last *odium generis humani*. In this way the image of the bourgeois has been boundlessly extended and carried further away toward the east with a fantastic, not only world-historical, but also metaphysical background. There it was able to give new life to the Russian hatred for the complication, artificiality, and intellectualism of Western European civilization, and in turn be reinvigorated by it. All the energies that had created this image were united on Russian soil. Both the Russian and the proletarian saw now in the bourgeois the incarnation of everything that sought to enslave life's art in a deadly mechanism.

This image migrated from the west to the east. But there it seized a myth for itself that no longer grew purely out of the instinct for class conflict, but contained strong nationalist elements. Sorel dedicated the last edition of his *Réflexions sur la violence* in 1919 to Lenin, as a kind of testament or apology.[23] He called him the greatest theorist of socialism since Marx and compared him as a statesman to Peter the Great. The difference was that today Russia no longer assimilated West European intellectualism, but on the contrary, the proletarian use of force here at least had reached its apotheosis—namely, that Russia again could be Russian, Moscow again the capital, and the

Europeanized upper classes who held their own land in contempt could be exterminated. Proletarian use of force had made Russia Muscovite again. In the mouth of an international Marxist that is remarkable praise, for it shows that the energy of nationalism is greater than the myth of class conflict.

Sorel's other examples of myth also prove that when they occur in the modern period, the stronger myth is national. The revolutionary wars of the French nation and the Spanish and German wars of liberation against Napoléon are symptoms of a national energy. In national feeling, various elements are at work in the most diverse ways, in very different peoples. The more naturalistic conceptions of race and descent, the apparently more typical *terrisme* of the celtic and romance peoples, the speech, tradition, and consciousness of a shared culture and education, the awareness of belonging to a community with a common fate or destiny, a sensibility of being different from other nations—all of that tends toward a national rather than a class consciousness today. Both can be combined—for example, in the friendship between Patrick Pearse, the martyr of the new Irish national consciousness and the Irish socialist Connolly, who both died victims of the Dublin rising of 1916.[24] A common spiritual enemy can also produce the most remarkable agreements; thus, for example, the Fascists' battle against Freemasonry parallels remarkably the Bolshevists' hatred of the Freemason, whom Trotsky called "the most perfidious deception of the working class by a radicalized bourgeoisie."[25] But wherever it comes to an open confrontation of the two myths, such as in Italy, the national myth has until today always been victorious. Italian Fascism depicted its communist enemy with a horrific face, the Mongolian face of Bolshevism; this has made a stronger impact and has evoked more powerful emotions than the socialist image of the bourgeois. Until now the democracy of mankind and parliamentarism has only once been contemptuously pushed aside through the conscious appeal to myth, and that was an example of the irrational power of the national myth. In his famous speech of

October 1922 in Naples before the March on Rome, Mussolini said, "We have created a myth, this myth is a belief, a noble enthusiasm; it does not need to be reality, it is a striving and a hope, belief and courage. Our myth is the nation, the great nation which we want to make into a concrete reality for ourselves."[26] In the same speech he called socialism an inferior mythology. Just as in the sixteenth century, an Italian has once again given expression to the principle of political realism. The meaning in intellectual history of this example is especially great because national enthusiasm on Italian soil has until now been based on democratic and constitutional parliamentary tradition and has appeared to be completely dominated by the ideology of Anglo-Saxon liberalism.

The theory of myth is the most powerful symptom of the decline of the relative rationalism of parliamentary thought. If anarchist authors have discovered the importance of the mythical from an opposition to authority and unity, then they have also cooperated in establishing the foundation of another authority, however unwillingly, an authority based on the new feeling for order, discipline, and hierarchy. Of course the abstract danger this kind of irrationalism poses is great. The last remnants of solidarity and a feeling of belonging together will be destroyed in the pluralism of an unforeseeable number of myths. For political theology that is polytheism, just as every myth is polytheistic. But as the strongest political tendency today, one cannot simply ignore it. Perhaps a parliamentary optimism still hopes even now that this movement can be relativized, and as in Fascist Italy, it will let all this happen around it, patiently waiting until discussion can be resumed. Perhaps discussion itself will be discussed, if there is only discussion. But the resumed discussion cannot content itself with repeating the question, "Parliamentarism, what else?"[27] and insist that at present there is no alternative. That argument would be irrelevant, one never capable of renewing the age of discussion.

Appendix: On the Ideology of Parliamentarism (1925)

Richard Thoma

The practical influence on politics which the ideological justification for any state form or governmental type exercises should surely not be exaggerated. It is always present to some extent in politics—even Marxist theory does not deny that—and under certain circumstances ideology can be a very important factor in historical events. Ideologists on the other hand are embedded in the general development of intellectual life, swept along and transformed by its currents. For that reason it is always imperative when investigating the contemporary circumstances and developmental possibilities of constitutional politics in Europe not to analyze the various ideologies of our times in isolation, drawing conclusions about their strength and vitality from the place they hold in intellectual history; this is especially true of the literary justifications for democracy, hereditary monarchy, parliamentarism, the dictatorship of the proletariat, the dictatorship of the strong man (whether justified by nationalism, cultural politics, or economic-eudaemonist considerations). In a very remarkable recent study by Carl Schmitt, professor of law and political science in Bonn, the ideological justifications for parliament and parliamentary government, the rationalist Marxist dictatorship, and the irrationalist dictatorship recommended by syndicalism that is currently being tested by Italian

Richard Thoma

Fascism have been treated in just this manner in an essay that is otherwise fascinating for its wealth of ideas. Although it is rewarding to extract the actual conclusions of this study, it must also be said at once that this is a very difficult business in which happy agreement and a negative critique very nearly counterbalance each other. Schmitt's text lacks, it seems to me, a coherent perspective. So far as a living whole can be divided into two rough halves at all, one could say this study is on the one hand a purely scientific contribution to our understanding of certain political ideas and their philosophical connections; the rest of it appears to be a kind of constitutional-political thesis and prognosis.

(a) This second aspect, which shall be dealt with first here, seems to me unsuccessful and inadequate. The intention of the author is not to repeat an already well-known and tiresome catalogue of the failings of modern parliamentary practice (p. 18ff.), but rather to explore "the ultimate core of the institution of modern parliament," from which it can be seen how far "this institution has lost its intellectual foundation and only remains standing as an empty apparatus." To the question (p. 33) "Why has parliament been in fact the *ultimum sapientiae* for many generations, and on what has the belief in this institution rested for over a century?" he gives the answer that the rationale for parliamentary institutions is not to be found in the familiar argument that the elected committee must function as a surrogate for an assembly of citizens that is no longer practically possible, as in what Smend has called the "dynamic-dialectic": "public deliberation of argument and counterargument, public debate and public discussion" in parliament and the free press. (p. 34). That was already expressed by others, for example, by Forçade (p. 103, note 49) and above all by Guizot. To this there is also joined the belief that through a free competition of opinions and aims, through discussion and public opinion, the "truth" can be discovered and parliament would thus be the defender of justice or at least of relatively better legislation and policies. Thus the "secret practices" of absolutism could be overcome; thus a government of law and justice might replace the rule of naked power. In that Schmitt discovers the "intellectual center" of modern parliamentarism in this ideology, he reaches the conclusion that parliamentarism has lost its historical-intellectual basis (p. 49), that it lacks any rationale today and is therefore dead and ready to collapse. It goes without saying that no rational person today is so naive and optimistic as to place any hope at all in such wonderful results from parliamentary debates and a free press.

Other theories opposed to the bourgeois ideal of peaceful negotiation and agreement are more intellectually alive today, in particular, the concept of a rationalistic dictatorship that springs from Marxist thought and certain "irrationalist theories of the direct use of force," whose most important theorist is Georges Sorel and whose most obvious practitioner today is Mussolini. Both extol a "myth": For the latter the myth is the nation's victorious tempest; for the former it is the myth of the general strike and socialism. The theory of a political myth is "the strongest expression of how much the relative rationalism of parliamentary thought has lost its persuasiveness" (p. 76).

That these opinions and conclusions end in a muddle scarcely needs to be said. The cause of the confusion is twofold. First of all the exposition is itself incomplete. If one wants to examine the foundations of an institution in intellectual history, one cannot confine oneself to the study of a single ideology that has been used to justify it. All of them must be included, and in our case one then quickly realizes that there are other and more important intellectual justifications for an elected representative assembly and for parliamentary government than Guizot's illusions. I cannot expand on this here, but one only needs to read, for example, the writings and speeches of Max Weber, Hugo Preuss, and Friedrich Naumann from the year 1917 onward to see that the political arguments with which they demanded a reform of the Reichstag and a transfer of constitutional power to its advantage were completely different, and that these are intellectually and in real political terms still very much alive. Instead of these Schmitt has picked out a single, and in fact completely "moldy," "intellectual basis of modern parliamentarism" and ignored all the rest.

To this something else must be added that is frequently disregarded in the literature of intellectual history: The worth and vitality of a political institution in no way depends on the quality and persuasiveness of the ideologies advanced for its justification. First, because books and articles can miss or ignore important arguments or events, but also because every institution "lives and develops" and goes through *metamorphoses of purpose and changes in structure*. It is, by the way, not entirely correct to say that no creative public discussion takes place any longer in modern parliament. There have only been changes in its structure. Creative *discussion* by parliamentarians has simply withdrawn into committees and the closed chambers of the parties or of the cabinet, into the interparty negotiations, and into discussions with experts and economic interests. *Open public* discussion in the plenum certainly means nothing for these but it continues to mean a great deal for the education of opinion outside parliament, in that it is read by journalists and other politicians and is consciously or unconsciously taken into consideration.

Perhaps Carl Schmitt is in danger of overemphasizing the literary appearances of things and is not always conscious that theoretical justifications for political institutions must be accepted with caution. They are not always true and seldom complete. Whoever supports the establishment or preservation of an institution certainly cannot often say, for instance, that he is only acting out of a pessimistic resignation or that he only defends something because it is the lesser evil; if he wants to be effective, he has to talk positively and awaken optimistic illusions, even believe in these himself, as long as he carries on the fight. If the illusions prove themselves deceptive afterward, an institution is still not, by a long way, finished because of that.

What Schmitt calls "the relative rationalism of parliamentary thought" has certainly "lost some of its obviousness." Even more than that, it has lost all its obviousness. Whoever pleads for the *ludi cartacei* of a representative assembly and its endowment with legislative powers as the choice of a government does so today for completely different constitutional, social-ethical considerations, hopes, and resignation than those found in Guizot and Forçade.

Further the syndicalist (class conflict) and Fascist (national) theory of myth is not "the strongest expression" that this obviousness has disappeared. The strongest expression of this is much more: In practice representatives intentionally belong to parties of the sort that enable election results to decide the most important policy of the nation in the first place, not parliament; also the theoretical perspective that political decisions are always voluntaristic, never intellectual, has now won general acceptance in intellectual history. The step from a belief in discussion to "decisionism" was taken long ago. The problem of our time is whether the decision should remain in the hands of a stable minority (the authoritarian state, or in the extreme, a dictatorship) or with a volatile, temporary minority (the party state); or whether certain social classes, be they proletarian or bourgeois, should be excluded or advantaged (the privilege state). It has by no means been proven that Europe is confronted by the dilemma: parliamentarism or dictatorship. Democracy has many other organizational possibilities than parliamentarism—though certainly not a monarchical one, just as certainly the republican one—if parliamentarism really should fail and could not regenerate itself. But a judgment about this is completely impossible today, even in England and France, not to mention Germany, where a youthful parliamentarism has scarcely learned to walk yet. The same is not true of the undemocratic state. Naturally it is possible that the constitutional politics of Europe will one day face the single alternative: democratic parliamentarism or a violent dictatorship. But that this is generally *actual*, I wager to deny in spite of Lenin, Mussolini, and Primo de Rivera.

(b) If I reject Schmitt's argument insofar as it declares the death of parliamentarism in intellectual terms, I can still speak of it as a clarification of relationships and connections in intellectual history with all the more admiration and agreement.

My praise is directed least toward the first two chapters, although they contain a wealth of sharp observations and instruction, for example, on the currently undeniable "obviousness of democratic legitimacy" and the readiness of the League of Nations to intervene on democratic grounds in the internal affairs of states. When the author argues in the first chapter, "Democracy and Parliamentarism," that the definition of democracy exhausts itself in a series of identifications (majority will is parliament's will, parliament's will is the people's will, and so on), then he confuses only one among many justifications for democracy, one that is certainly the most prominent in the literature but hardly the most important among the historical factors in European democratization. In terms of *Realpolitik*, nationalistic, power-political (Konnex with universal conscription), tactical (Disraeli, Bismarck), social-political arguments for democratization have been more important than the ideal of freedom and equality. I have already indicated the one-sidedness of chapter 2, "The Principles of Parliamentarism." There remains only to say that the weaknesses in Schmitt's argument are overshadowed by the equally learned and profound analysis of Guizot's ideology, locating it in the intellectual world of liberalism, with its belief in balance and harmony, and in the philosophical principles of the Englightenment.

The sympathy of the author is with the "irrationalism of the mythical," which in spite of its origins in anarchism has worked to reconstruct the foundation for "a new feeling for order, hierarchy, and discipline." But he sees and fears its risks, which are not—naturally—of a practical sort but also intellectual. These he discovers in the possibility of a destructive pluralism of myths, a "polytheism." I would hazard to guess, but not assert, that behind these ultimately rather sinister observations there stands the unexpressed personal conviction of the author that an alliance between a nationalistic dictator and the Catholic Church could be the real solution and achieve a definitive restoration of order, discipline, and hierarchy. Regarding this conjecture it should again be said that he seems completely blind to the fact that there is a third "myth" in our time, no less vital than the national and revolutionary myths, and the only one compatible with the Christian ethic and with which the Catholic Church has often allied itself: the myth of perpetual peace through self-determination and democracy. The irrationality of the spiritual foundations and chiliastic goal of this myth is not limited because in the circumstances of contemporary Europe it points in the same direction as that of the rational considerations and bourgeois good sense.

Notes

Preface to the Second Edition (1926)

1. [Tr.] "Die Geistesgeschichtliche Lage des heutigen Parlamentarismus" first appeared in the *Bonner Festgabe für Ernst Zitelmann* (Munich & Leipzig: Duncker & Humblot, 1923), 415–473. This first edition comprised the text from the introduction through chapter 4; the preface, "On the Contradiction between Parliamentarism and Democracy," first appeared as "Der Gegensatz von Parlamentarismus und Moderner Massendemokratie," *Hochland* 23 (1926), 257–270, in response to Richard Thoma's critique "Zur Ideologie des Parlamentarismus und der Diktatur," which had appeared the previous year in the *Archiv für Sozialwissenschaft und Sozialpolitik* 53 (1925), 212–217. The preface was reprinted under its original title in Schmitt's *Positionen und Begriffe im Kampf mit Weimar, Genf, Versailles, 1923–39* (Hamburg: Hanseatische Verlag, 1940), 52–66.

2. Richard Thoma, "Zur Ideologie des Parlamentarismus," and in Kurt Kluxen, ed., *Parlamentarismus* (Königstein/Ts: Verlagsgruppe Athenäum, Hain, Scripter, Hanstein, 1980), 54–58.

3. [Tr.] See the translation of Thoma's review included in this volume. Largely because of his *Römischer Katholizismus und politische Form* (1923), Schmitt was the best-known advocate of the Catholic view among German jurists at this time. See Karl Muth's review of *Römischer Katholizismus*: "Zeitgeschichte," *Hochland* 21 (1923) 96–100. Muth states its main thesis accurately: "In contrast to Cromwell's rage [against Roman Catholicism], its opponent in the modern age has become more and more rationalistic, humanitarian, utilitarian, and superficial . . . but as many degrees of anti-Catholic feeling as there have been, there still remains the fear of Roman Catholicism's incomprehensible political power" (p. 96). Schmitt understood these anti-Roman tendencies as a "depoliticization" of the world in which "order [would be] secured through the play of economic and

technical forces." In contrast to this depoliticization Schmitt saw the church as "the protector of political form as such." The church, according to Muth, is entitled to "call nations to order" when they offend against natural or divine law. For a much later attack on "Catholic dictatorship"—the chancellorship of Heinrich Brüning—see Carl von Ossietzsky, "Katholische Diktator," *Die Weltbühne* 27 (1931), 481–487. On Schmitt's Catholic education and cultural inheritance see Joseph W. Bendersky, *Carl Schmitt: Theorist for the Reich* (Princeton: Princeton University Press, 1983), 3ff.

4. [Tr.] On the French "doctrinaire liberal" tradition see Luis Diez del Corral, *Doktrinärer Liberalismus. Guizot und sein Kreis* (Neuwied am Rhein & Berlin: Luchterhand, 1964). On the Benthamite tradition and Mill see Frederick Rosen, *Jeremy Bentham and Representative Democracy: A Study of the Constitutional Code* (Oxford: Oxford University Press, 1983); and Joseph Hamburger, *Intellectuals in Politics: John Stuart Mill and the Philosophical Radicals* (New Haven: Yale University Press, 1965). On Burke and the English conservative tradition of representative thought see Alfred Cobban, *Edmund Burke and the Revolt against the Eighteenth Century* (London: George Allen and Unwin, 1929). It is not clear which of the texts by Burke, Bentham, Mill, and Guizot Schmitt had in mind here; he only makes specific reference to Bentham's "On the Liberty of the Press and Public Discussion" (1821) and Guizot's *Histoire des origines du gouvernement représentatif en France* (1851). Schmitt would probably have known Burke's *Reflections on the Revolution in France* (1790) and J. S. Mill's *On Liberty* (1859), whose account of parliamentary reason he appears to have taken over; he may also have known Mill's *Representative Government* (1861).

5. [Tr.] Schmitt's reference to the revolutions of 1848 already indicates that the conflict that he asserts exists between democracy and parliamentarism is the result of social change in Europe. In France the revolution was directed against a bourgeois parliamentary government. Lorenz von Stein, *Geschichte der soziale Bewegung im Frankreich von 1789 bis auf unsere Tage* (Leipzig: Wigand, 1850), 3 vols. Cf. Carl Schmitt, "Die Stellung Lorenz von Stein in der Geschichte des 19. Jahrhundert," *Schmollers Jahrbuch* 64 (1940), 641–646.

6. An absolutely typical example is the definition of parliamentarism in the book by Gaetano Mosca, *Teorica dei Governi e Governo Parlamentare* (Milan, 1925), 147; by *parliamentarism* he understands a government in which political superiority in the state belongs to elements chosen, directly or indirectly, through elections. The popular equation of a representative constitution and parliamentarism also contains this mistake. [Schmitt's reference is to the second edition. *Teorica dei Governi e Governo* was first published in 1884 (Rome: Ermanno Loescher, 1884) —*tr.*]

7. [Tr.] Schmitt refers to Italian Fascism. The term *Fascism* is taken from the Italian *fascio* (bund or bundle) and *fasces*, in Latin the ancient symbol of governmental authority. First used to designate a political movement in Italy under Benito Mussolini (1922–1943)— to which Schmitt refers in this text when he mentions Fascism—the word later became a collective term for nationalistic, antidemocratic, and antiliberal reaction in Europe. See Carl Schmitt's review of Erwin von Beckerath's *Wesen und Werden des faschistischen Staates*, in *Schmollers Jahrbuch* 53 (1929), 107–113. The Bolshevists were at first only a faction in the 1917 revolution in Russia, led by Lenin and Trotsky. At the All-Soviet Congress, they had fewer delegates (108) than the Mensheviks (248) and Social Democrats

(255). After Kerensky's Social Democratic government moved against them in July 1917, a radicalization in St. Petersburg and Moscow strengthened the Bolshevik position and in October 1917 a coup d'état, masterminded by Trotsky, overthrew the Kerensky regime and issued in "a completely new form of popular representation that did not follow parliamentary principles and which only expressed the view of the proletariat." The quote is from Georg von Rauch, "Sowjetrussland von der Oktoberrevolution bis zum Sturz Chruschows, 1917–1964," in Theodor Schieder, ed., *Handbuch der europäischen Geschichte*, vol. 7, pt. 1 (Stuttgart: Unions Verlag, 1959), 483. At the time Schmitt wrote, the term *Bolshevist* referred not only to the Russian regime under Lenin but also to radical working-class politics in general, and was loosely used by the middle classes to refer to almost any sort of countercultural or anarchist tendency. This ordinary use of *Bolshevist* has roughly the same connotations as the term *communist* does today.

8. [Tr.] Cf. Karl Beyerle, *Parlamentarisches System — oder was sonst?* (Munich: Pfeiffer & Co., Verlag, 1921), mentioned by Schmitt.

9. [Tr.] Article 21 of the Weimer constitution reads: "The Members of the Reichstag are representatives of the entire nation. They are bound only to their consciences and are not bound by any instructions." The other liberal freedoms mentioned by Schmitt were also incorporated in the constitution. Article 29 ("The Reichstag acts openly") declared the principle of openness, and a closed sitting required a petition from fifty members and a two-thirds majority. Members also enjoyed parliamentary immunity according to article 36: "No member of the Reichstag or of a Landtag may, at any time, because of his vote or because of opinions expressed in the course of performing his duties, be juridically or officially prosecuted or in any other way made to answer outside the Assembly." See Horst Hildebrandt, ed., *Die deutschen Verfassungen des 19. und 20. Jahrhunderts* (Paderborn: Schöningh, 1979), 69ff. On the theory of representation see Gerhard Leibholz, *Das Wesen der Representation* (Berlin: Walter de Gruyter & Co., 1929), and Schmitt's critique in *Verfassungslehre* (Munich & Leipzig: Duncker & Humblot, 1928), 240ff. and 212ff. On the social function of political representation see Rudolf Smend, "Integration durch Representation," in his *Verfassung und Verfassungsrecht* (1928) and reprinted in *Staatsrechtliche Abhandlungen und andere Aufsätze* (Berlin: Duncker & Humblot, 1955, 1968), 119–276; and Schmitt's critique in *Verfassungslehre*, 207ff.

10. [Tr.] Montesquieu, *L'Esprit des lois* (1748); translated as *The Spirit of the Laws* (Chicago: Encyclopedia Britannica, 1952).

11. [Tr.] On the role of Weber, Preuss, and Naumann see my introduction to this volume.

12. [Tr.] On the German reception of English parliamentary theory see Robert Redslob, *Die parlamentarische Regierung in ihrer echten und in ihren unechten Form* (Tübingen: Mohr, 1918), and Max Weber's discussion of the English system in "Parlament und Regierung im neugeordneten Deutschland," in Johannes Winckelmann, ed., *Max Weber. Gesammelte Politische Schriften* (Tübingen: Mohr, 1980), 353ff. See also Ludwig Bergsträsser, "Die Entwicklung des Parlamentarismus in Deutschland," in Kluxen, ed., *Parlamentarismus*, 138–160.

13. [Tr.] M. J. Bonn, *Die Krisis der europäischen Demokratie* (Tübingen: Mohr, 1925). This book is noted with Alfred Weber's *Die Krise des modernen Staatsgedankens in Europa* (Stuttgart: Deutsche Verlags Anstalt, 1925) in the *Berichte* for 1925–26 of the Deutsche Hochschule für Politik as "parallel" works; both analyze antidemocratic and antiparliamentary movements in the 1920s. The anonymous reviewer concluded that Bonn's work was the better and more objective of the two: see *Zeitschrift für Politik* 15 (1926), 31.

14. [Tr.] See Edmund Burke, *Thoughts on the Cause of the Present Discontents (1770)*; see also Schmitt's discussion of Gentz in *Politische Romantik* (Munich & Leipzig: Duncker & Humblot, 1919), 13ff. Gentz, whom Schmitt calls Metternich's journalistic clerk, translated Burke and Mounier into German and was the author of several counterrevolutionary tracts and histories: *Fragmente aus der Geschichte des politischen Gleichgewichts Europa* (1804); *Über den politischen Zustand Europas vor und nach der französischen Revolution* (1801–1802); *Betrachtung über den Ursprung und Charakter des Krieges gegen die französische Revolution* (1907). On the reception of Burke's ideas in Germany see Ursula Vogel, *Konservativer Kritik der bürgerlichen Revolution. August Wilhelm Rehberg* (Neuwied am Rhein & Berlin: Luchterhand, 1972).

15. [Tr.] Political parties had no constitutional status in the Republic; like the constitution of the United States, the Weimar constitution did not mention them, and certain of its provisions could even be interpreted as barriers to the functioning of modern political parties in the state. Nevertheless, "the Weimar Republic had developed into a 'party state' precisely because the parties elevated themselves, through the socially subordinate organs of the state's will, into principal organs of governmental power and thereby to direct factors in the state." See E. R. Huber, *Deutsche Verfassungsgeschichte seit 1789*, vol. 6 (Stuttgart: Verglag W. Kohlhammer, 1981), 135. See also Sigmund Neumann, *Die deutschen Parteien. Wesen und Wandel nach dem Krieg* (Berlin: Verlag Junker & Dünnhaupt, 1932), and Ludwig Bergsträsser, *Geschichte der politischen Parteien im Deutschland* (Mannheim, Berlin, & Leipzig: J. Bensheimer, 1924).

16. Walter Lippmann, *Public Opinion* (London: George Allen & Unwin, 1922). A recently published book—interesting, witty, and important despite all its leaps of thought is Wyndham Lewis, *The Art of Being Ruled* (London: Chatto & Windus, 1922). Lewis explains the transition from the intellectual to the affective and sensual through modern democracy, which initiates a general "feminization" that suppresses the manly.

17. But in this respect a remark made by Robert Michels in the foreword to the second edition of his *Soziologie des Parteiwesens* (Leipzig: Alfred Kröner Verlag, 1926) is exactly appropriate: "In the area of theoretical, but also applied, mass psychology German social science is a few decades behind the French, Italian, American, and English" (p. xviii). It only remains to be said that a book such as Michels's, with its astonishing wealth of material and thought, would certainly be well suited to compensate for a decade's backlog. [In this passage Michels not only notes that social science in Germany has remained far behind that of other countries but also connects the Germans' lack of theoretical interest to their political culture: "Investigations into the character and concept of party life and leadership seemed bizarre from the start to the dominant conservative tendency in German intellectual life. The German socialists were for their part certainly a mass party but their great strength lay in this concept remaining

unexamined. Finally democrats, whether bourgeois or radical, prove themselves just as suspicious, ticklish, and easly offended when it comes to investigations of the problem of leadership as the bourgeoisie is when it comes to analysis of private property and profit. . . . To these a third thing must be added: The German national character with its overestimation of organizational factors must feel very painfully touched by this critique of the nature of political parties, as if things particularly valuable and central to it had been attacked." Michels remarks in this foreword on the increased interest throughout Europe, during and after the war, in the complex of questions raised by his work, and he notes the appearance of Schmitt's *Parlamentarismus* in the Ernst Zitelman Festschrift (1923). See Michels, *Soziologie des Parteiwesens*, xix–xx; translated as *Political Parties: A Sociological Study of the Oligarchical Tendency of Modern Democracy* (New York: Free Press, 1962). The English and American social science literature seldom brings Michels's work into its historical context or compares it with other contemporary works to which Michels refers, such as Oswald Spengler's *Der Untergang des Abendlandes. Umriss einer Morphologie der Weltgeschichtliche* (1922–23) and Sigmund Freud's *Massenpsychologie und Ich-Analyse* (1921). —tr.]

18. [Tr.] Comte de Cavour was an enthusiastic follower of Benjamin Constant and François Guizot, and supported the bourgeois revolution of 1830 that overthrew Charles X. Elected to parliament in July 1848, Cavour became finance minister in 1850.

19. [Tr.] For a lucid discussion of Bentham's views on parliamentary government and publicity, see Rosen, *Jeremy Bentham and Representative Democracy*.

20. [Tr.] Prévost-Paradol was a friend and classmate of Taine's at the École Normale. He contributed political articles to the *Journal des Débats* and wrote three volumes of occasional pieces on public issues during the 1850s and 1860s (*Essais de politique et de literature*).

21. [Tr.] The phrase is Harold Laski's: "The fundamental hypothesis of government in a representative system is that it is government by discussion." See Laski, "The Problem of Administrative Areas," in *Foundations of Sovereignty* (New York: Harcourt, Brace & Co., 1921), 36.

22. [Tr.] The archetypal bourgeois king was Louis-Philippe. See Alfred Cobban, *A History of Modern France*, vol. 2 (Harmondsworth: Penguin, 1961), 133ff., and Karl Marx, "The Eighteenth Brumaire of Louis Bonaparte" (1852), in Karl Marx and Friedrich Engels, *Selected Works in Three Volumes* (Moscow: Progress Publishers, 1977), 394–487.

23. [Tr.] Cf. Aristotle, *Politics* (1280a): "In democracies . . . justice is considered to mean equality. . . . It does mean equality—but equality for those who are equal, and not for all." See also the *Ethics* (1137б) on equity.

24. [Tr.] Cf. Hermann Heller's "Politische Demokratie und soziale Homogenität" (1928), in Heller, *Gesammelte Schriften*, ed. Christoph Müller, vol. 2 (Leiden: Sijthoff, 1971), 421–433, and the discussion of Heller in my introduction.

25. [Tr.] A transfer of Greek and Turkish populations in southeastern Europe was agreed to in the Treaty of Lausanne (November 21, 1922) and began in 1923; 1.2 million

Greeks were transferred from Asia Minor to the Greek mainland and 330,000 Turks were sent from Macedonia, Thessalonika, and Epirus to Turkey. For a description of the hardship involved see Winthrop D. Lane, "Why Greeks and Turks Oppose Being 'Exchanged,' " *Current History* 18 (1923), 86–90.

26. [Tr.] From the early nineteenth century Australian law excluded certain immigrants on racial grounds. The policy of maintaining a "white Australia" was justified on the grounds of Australia's geographical location and its historic ties to Britain; Asians were the principal target group. This policy was defended in a study by Myrna Willard, *A History of the White Australia Policy* (Melbourne: University of Melbourne Press, 1923). She writes, "National self-preservation is the object of the policy. Australians feared that non-European immigration . . . might radically alter, perhaps destroy, the British character of the community. They knew that racial unity, though not necessarily racial homogeneity, was essential for national unity, for the national life. The union of a people depends on common loyalty to common ideals. . . . To preserve the unity of their national life, a people can admit emigrants from alien races only if within a reasonable time they show a willingness and a capacity to amalgamate ideally as well as racially with them. Australians have formed their restrictive policy because, through their own experience and the experience of other countries, they believed that at present non-Europeans of the labouring classes have neither this willingness nor this capacity" (pp. 189–190). Further, "a restrictive policy seemed to conflict with the conception of the brotherhood of man and with the democratic ideal of the equality of all . . . [but] Australians felt that it was ultimately in the interests of the British Empire itself" (pp. 205–206).

27. [Tr.] "The English Commonwealth was in form a democracy, as compared with most republics then existing, but in substance it was an oligarchy, half-religious, half-military" [F. C. Montague, *The History of England: From the Accession of James I to the Restoration (1603–1660)* (London: Longmans, Green & Co., 1907)]. On the Puritan sects and the democratic theory of John Lilburne see William Haller, *Liberty and Reformation in the Puritan Revolution* (New York: Columbia University Press, 1955).

28. The political substance that belongs to democracy can certainly not be found in economics. Political homogeneity does not follow from economic equality; to be sure, great economic inequalities can play a—negative—role in destroying or endangering political homogenity. The further development of this thesis belongs to another context.

29. [Tr.] Thoma argues that democracy requires universal suffrage; see my introduction to this volume.

30. [Tr.] "It is true that Arabs could acquire, by naturalization, all the rights of French citizens; all they had to do was abandon their status in Moslem law, adopt monogamy, accept the full principles of the civil code: in short, by their standards, cease to be Moslems. Few were willing to pay this price" [D. W. Brogan, *The Development of Modern France (1870–1939)* (London: Hamish Hamilton, 1967), 222]. John R. Seeley (an exponent of the "Greater Britain" idea) wrote that India could not be part of Greater Britain in the same sense as "tens of millions" of Englishmen who lived outside the British Isles could be; on this strain of British imperial thought see John S. Galbraith, "The Empire

since 1783," in Robin W. Winks, *The Historiography of the British Empire-Commonwealth* (Durham: Duke University Press, 1966).

31. At least in this respect, a "pluralism" exists. For the social pluralism into which contemporary democracies of mankind will dissolve, according to the prognosis of M. J. Bonn in *Die Krisis der europäischen Demokratie* (1925), another, more effective form already exists and has always existed.

32. The distinction (between democracy and liberalism) has been very successfully brought out in an essay by Werner Becker ["Demokratie und Massenstaat"] in the journal [*Die*] *Schildgenossen* (September 1925) [459–478]. It is based on an excellent paper read at my politics seminar during the summer semester, 1925. Herman Hefele's article ["Demokratie und Liberalismus"] in *Hochland* (November 1924) [34–43] also emphasizes the distinction between liberalism and democracy. Nevertheless I maintain, in contrast to Becker and Hefele, that the definition of democracy is an identity of governed and governing.

33. [Tr.] Jean-Jacques Rousseau, *Du contrat social* (1762); English translation by Maurice Cranston, *The Social Contract* (Harmondsworth: Penguin, 1968). Cf. Schmitt's review of C. E. Vaughn's *Studies in the History of Political Philosophy before and after Rousseau* (London: Longmans, Green & Co., 1925) in the *Deutsche Literatur-Zeitung* 46 (1925), 2086–2090.

34. Alfred Weber, *Die Krise des modernen Staatsgedankens in Europa* (1925).

35. Carl Brinkmann, "Carl Schmitt's *Politische Romantik*," *Archiv für Sozialwissenschaft und Sozialpolitik* 54 (1925), 533.

36. [Tr.] "Ce mot de *Finance* est un mot d'esclave; il est inconnu dans la cité." *Du contrat social*, Bk. III, chap. 15, sect. 3.

37. "On doit concevoir . . . faute d'un interet commun qui unisse et identifie la regle du juge avec celle de la partie." *Du contrat social*, Bk. II, chap. 4, sect. 7.

38. [Tr.] Weber, *Krise des modernen Staatsgedankens*.

39. [Tr.] "To the concept of God in the seventeenth and eighteenth centuries belonged the idea of the transcendence of God over the world, as the transcendence of the sovereign over the state belonged to its state philosophy. In the nineteenth century everything became increasingly dominated by conceptions of immanence. All the identities that recur repeatedly in the political theory and jurisprudence of the nineteenth century rest on such conceptions of immanence: the democratic thesis about the identity of the governed and the governing; the organized state theory and its identity of the state and sovereignty; the jurisprudence of Krabbe and its identification of sovereignty with the positive law, and finally Kelsen's theory of the identity of the state with the system of positive law" [Schmitt, *Politische Theologie* (Munich & Leipzig: Duncker & Humblot, 1922), 63]. On legal positivism see my introduction to this volume.

40. Pufendorf, *De jure naturae et gentium* (1672), Bk. VII, chap. 6, sect. 8. [A two-volume edition of the original text and an English translation was published by the Clarendon

Press in 1934. Schmitt refers to the chapter "On the Characteristics of Supreme Sovereignty" and the following passage: "But in aristocracies and democracies, where there are some who command and some who obey, and when therefore the latter can secure some rights from the promises and pacts of the former, there is clearly to be seen a difference between absolute and limited sovereignty" (vol. 2, p. 1065). —tr.]

41. [Tr.] See note 13, above.

42. [Tr.] Article 125 of the Weimar constitution stated: "The freedom and the secrecy of the ballot are guaranteed." Reich and Länder legislation defined this provision further. See Gerhard Anschütz, *Die Verfassung des deutschen Reichs vom 11 August 1919* (Berlin: Stilke Verlag, 1928), 332-333.

43. [Tr.] Schmitt quotes from the second sentence of the Weimar constitution; see Anschütz, *Die Verfassung des deutschen Reichs*, 36ff., on the meaning of the sentence "All state power comes from the people."

Introduction to the First Edition (1923)

1. [Tr.] On the political theory of the counterrevolution in Carl Schmitt's thought see the chapter "Zur Staatsphilosophie der Gegenrevolution (de Maistre, Bonald, Donoso-Cortés)," in *Politische Theologie* (Munich & Leipzig: Duncker & Humblot, 1922), 67-84, and Carl Schmitt, *Donoso Cortés in gesamteuropäischer Interpretation: Vier Aufsätze* (Cologne: Greven Verlag, 1950).

2. [Tr.] *Atti parlamentari della Camera dei Deputati*, November 26, 1922.

3. [Tr.] H. Berthélemy, *Traité élémentaire de droit administratif* (Paris: Rousseau, 1923, 10th edition).

4. Of the many German publications on this subject only a few shall be named: M. J. Bonn, *Die Auflösung des modernen Staats* (Berlin, 1921), and *Die Krisis der europäischen Demokratie* (Tübingen, 1925); K. Beyerle, *Parlamentarisches System—oder was sonst?* (Munich, 1921); Carl Landauer, "Sozialismus und parlamentarisches System," *Archiv für Sozialwissenshaft und Sozialpolitik* 48 (1922), and "Die Wege zur Eroberung des demokratischen Staats durch die Wirtschaftsleiter," in [M. Palyi, ed.,] *Erinnerungsgabe für Max Weber* (1922), vol. 2, and "Die Ideologie des Wirtschaftsparlamentarismus," in [Bonn and Palyi, eds.,] *Festgabe für L. Brentano* (1925), vol. 1, 153ff.; R. Thoma, "Der Begriff der modernen Demokratie in seinem Verhältnis zum Staatsbegriff," in [Palyi, ed.,] *Erinnerungsgabe für Max Weber* (1922), vol. 2 [cf. Carl Schmitt, *Archiv für Sozialwissenschaft und Sozialpolitik*, 51 (1924)], and "Zur Ideologie des Parlamentarismus und der Diktatur," *Archiv für Sozialwissenschaft und Sozialpolitik*, 53 (1925); Heinz Marr, "Klasse und Partei in der modernen Demokratie," in *Frankfurter gelehrte Reden und Abhandlungen* (1925) [cf. E. Rosenbaum, *Hamburgerischen Wirtschaftsdienst*, February 26, 1926]; Karl Löwenstein, *Minderheitsregierung in Grossbritannien* (Munich, 1925); Hermann Port, "Zweiparteiensystem und Zentrum,"

Hochland (July 1925); W. Lambach, *Die Herrschaft der 500* (Hamburg, 1926); Ernst Müller-Meiningen, *Parlamentarismus* (Berlin, 1926). On the perspective of Oswald Spengler, see the summary and overview by Otto Koellreutter, *Die Staatslehre Oswald Spenglers* (Jena, 1924). From the extensive literature on the "corporations" (*berufsständischen*) problem see Heinrich Herrfahrdt, *Das Problem der berufsständischen Vertretung* (Berlin, 1921), and Edgar Tatarin-Tarnheyden, "Kopfzahldemokratie: Organishe Demokratie und Oberhausproblem," *Zeitschrift für Politik*, 15 (1926), 97ff.; Heinz Brauweiler, *Berufsstand und Staat* (Berlin, 1925), and his "Parlamentarismus and berufsständische Politik," *Preussische Jahrbücher*, 202 (1925), and the critical discussion by Carl Landauer noted above. On the particular difficulties of parliament in relation to the modern economy, see Heinrich Göppert, *Staat und Wirtschaft* (Tübingen, 1924).

5. [Tr.] Schmitt's reference is not specific. Cf. Jacob Burckhardt, *Briefe*, ed. Max Burckhardt (Basel: Schwabe & Co., Verlag, 1949-63), 5 vols.

6. [Tr.] Moisei Ostrogorski, *La Démocratie et l'organisation de partis politique* (Paris: Calmann-Lévy, 1903); Seymour Martin Lipset, ed., *Democracy and the Organization of Political Parties* (New Brunswick, N.J.: Transaction Books, 1982). Hillaire Belloc and Cecil Chesterton, *The Party System* (London: Stephen Swift, 1911); Robert Michels, *Soziologie des Parteiwesens* (Leipzig: Alfred Kröner Verlag, 1926), and *Political Parties* (New York: Free Press, 1962).

1 Democracy and Parliamentarism

1. [Tr.] On German political thought in the last century, see James J. Sheehan, *German Liberalism in the Nineteenth Century* (London: Methuen, 1982), and Heinrich A. Winkler, *Preussischer Liberalismus und deutscher Nationalstaat* (Tübingen: Mohr, 1964). A fierce controversy was set off in 1980-1981 by Geoffrey Eley and David Blackbourne, *Mythen deutscher Geschichtsschreibung* (Berlin: Ullstein, 1980). Blackbourne and Eley attacked the thesis of a German *Sonderweg*: that while all other European countries (especially England) had become more democratic in the course of the nineteenth century, Germany took a "special route" to modernity—a modern industry but a feudal state and political system. While the authors' intention was at least partly to criticize the supposed genius of English political development, which some German historians hold up as a standard by which German historical development should be measured, the Blackbourne-Eley thesis echoes Carl Schmitt. They, like Schmitt, have discovered an identity between "democracy" and "liberalism" in nineteenth-century political thought, which they are unwilling (on supposedly different grounds) to admit. Winkler, whom they charge with equating the advance of the bourgeoisie and the development of democratic forms, has rightly answered: "None of the German historians criticized by Blackbourne and Eley would have thought to blur the distinction between 'liberals' and 'democrats.' " Winkler, "Der deutsche Sonderweg: Eine Nachlese," *Merkur*, 8 (1981), 793-804. Cf. Winkler's careful distinction of political currents in nineteenth-century German political thought and politics in his *Preussischer Liberalismus*, 22ff. and 93.

2. [Tr.] Ranke "feared the democratic and revolutionary tendencies within the nationalist movement, which, in his view, threatened the continued existence of European cultural

life." Rudolf Vierhaus, "Ranke und die Anfänge der deutsche Geschichtswissenschaft," in Bernd Faulenbach, ed., *Geschichtswissenschaft im Deutschland* (Munich: Beck, 1974). Cf. Theodore H. von Laue, *Leopold Ranke: The Formative Years* (Princeton: Princeton University Press, 1950).

3. [Tr.] "The immediate future of European society is completely democratic" [Alexis de Tocqueville, *Journeys to England and Ireland*, quoted in George Watson, *The English Ideology: Studies in the Language of Victorian Politics* (London: Allen Lane, 1973), 155]. See also Tocqueville's *Democracy in America* (1835), where a profound pessimism about the conformity of American society is expressed: Alexis de Tocqueville, *De la démocratie en Amérique* (Paris, 1835); translated as *Democracy in America*, ed. J. P. Mayer and Max Lehrner (New York: Harper & Row, 1966).

4. On this see the excellent work by Kathleen Murray, *Taine und die englische Romantik* (Munich & Leipzig, 1924). [Kathleen Murray's study of Taine and the English Romantics was dedicated to Carl Schmitt and published by Duncker & Humblot. She writes in her introduction that Taine was "one of the greatest and most representative men of the 19th century," who as a critic and historian "combined all the enormous contradictions and inconsistencies of his age within himself." Murray conceived Taine's work under both aesthetic and sociological perspectives, and it is clear that she was much influenced by Schmitt's *Politische Romantik* (1919). The theme of the second part of *Taine und die englische Romantik* allows one to establish a mutual influence; she deals with Taine's perception that "a new public belongs to every new work of art" and that the specific audience (*Publikum*) of romantic art is "a bourgeois, plebiscitary public" (Murray, 65). Carl Schmitt's description of Guizot's influence and assessment of democracy paraphrases Murray's discussion of "Das politische Ideal" (53ff.). See also her chapter "Die Typen des Engländers und des Bourgeois" (67ff.) and the comment—as valid for her own and parts of Carl Schmitt's work as for Taine's—that "Taine . . . always wanted to describe general 'types' and looked for firm but not measurable relationships between facts and groups of facts which make up social and moral life. . . . He wants to achieve an 'ideal type' as the zoologists understand it. . . . These relationships he calls laws (*lois*) and says that Montesquieu wanted to discover nothing else" (ibid., 6). See also Hippolyte Taine, *Histoire de la littérature anglaise* (Paris: 1863); François Pierre Guillaume Guizot, *De la démocratie en France* (Paris: Victor Masson, 1849), and *L'Eglise et la société chrétienne en 1861* (Paris: Michel Levy, 1861). —tr.]

5. [Tr.] Walter Schotte, in the *Preussische Jahrbücher*, 181 (1920), 136–137, commented that "English conservatives have never been lacking in political insight"; unlike German politicians, English Tories knew when to introduce reforms that would conserve their own position. Schotte refers to the minority government of Derby-Disraeli, which introduced the reform bill that had been the immediate cause of the fall of the Liberal government under Gladstone, which Disraeli's replaced. On Disraeli see Maurice Cowling, *Disraeli, Gladstone and the Revolution: The Passing of the Second Reform Bill, 1867* (Cambridge: Cambridge University Press, 1967). Keith Middlemas, *Politics in Industrial Society: The Experience of the British System since 1911* (London: Andre Deutsch, 1979), provides an often provocative view of English political culture in this century; see especially "Party and Parliamentary Illusion," 307ff., and "A Crisis of the State?", 430ff.

6. [Tr.] On the development of German Social Democracy see C. E. Schorske, *German Social Democracy, 1905–1917* (Cambridge, Mass.: Harvard University Press, 1955).

7. [Tr.] On Switzerland as a conservative democracy see Benjamin R. Barber, *Death of Communal Liberty: A History of Freedom in a Swiss Mountain Canton* (Princeton: Princeton University Press, 1974). In addition to Marx's "Eighteenth Brumaire of Louis Bonaparte" (1852), see the following histories of France under Napoleon III: Theodor Zeldin, *Emile Ollivier and the Liberal Empire of Napoleon III* (Oxford: Clarendon Press, 1963), and *The Political System of Napoleon III* (London: Macmillan & Co., 1958); H. C. Payne, *The Police-State of Louis Napoleon-Bonaparte, 1851–1860* (Seattle: University of Washington Press, 1966).

8. [Tr.] A classic exposition of English "guild socialism" can be found in G. D. H. Cole's *Guild Socialism Restated* (London: Leonard Parsons, 1920). Cole argued that "theoretical democracy" was rendered largely "inoperative" by "the substitution of the representative for the represented in representative democracy" (13–14). He demanded that the concept of democracy be extended beyond a "narrowly 'political' sense" to include social and economic organization as well: "No amount of electoral machinery on a basis of 'one man, one vote' will make [the rich man and the wage slave] really equal socially or politically" (15).

9. [Tr.] Max Weber, "Parlament und Regierung im neugeordneten Deutschland" (1918), in Johannes Winckelmann, ed., *Max Weber. Gesammelte Politische Schriften* (Tübingen: Mohr, 1980), 306–443; Keith Tribe, trans., "Parliament and Government in Newly Organized Germany" *Economy and Society*, 4 (1983), 1381–1462.

10. [Tr.] Hans Kelsen, *Wesen und Wert der Demokratie* (Tübingen: Mohr, 1929, 2d edition). First published in the *Archiv für Sozialwissenschaft und Sozialpolitik*, 47 (1920), 50–85.

11. Rousseau, *Du contrat social*, Bk. IV, chap. 2, sect. 8.

12. [Tr.] See Locke's discussion of the origins of political societies in chapter 8 of the Second Treatise. John Locke, *Two Treatises of Government* (Cambridge: Cambridge University Press, 1970), 348ff.

13. [Tr.] Rousseau, *Du contrat social*, Bk. IV, chap. 2, sect. 8.

14. [Tr.] This is a reference to the German revolution that began in November 1918. See A. J. Ryder, *The German Revolution of 1918* (Cambridge: Cambridge University Press, 1967), and the fluent discussion of this period by Völker Berghahn, "War and Civil War, 1914–1923," in his *Modern Germany: Society, Economy, and Politics in the Twentieth Century* (Cambridge: Cambridge University Press, 1982), 38–81. On the *republicains de la veille* see Lorenz von Stein, *Geschichte der sociale Bewegung im Frankreich* (Leipzig: Wigand, 1850), which Schmitt knew well.

15. *The Clarke Papers* [ed. C. H. Firth], vol. 2 (London: The Camden Society, 1794).

16. [Tr.] Carl Schmitt, *Legalität und Legitimität* (Munich & Leipzig: Duncker & Humblot, 1932), argued that "unconstitutional parties" (the KPD and NSDAP) should not enjoy

an "equal chance" to come to power in the state because they were committed to destroying the substance of the constitution. Cf. Joseph W. Bendersky, *Carl Schmitt: Theorist for the Reich* (Princeton: Princeton University Press, 1983), 144ff.

17. Very informative on the democratic dialectic is Lorenz von Stein, *Die socialistischen und communistischen Bewegungen, 1848*, Appendix, 25–26. [Schmitt refers to Stein's appendices "Briefe über Frankreich." The argument of the fourth letter, "Die Kammer," clearly influenced Schmitt's conception of parliamentarism. Stein writes about the French parliament in May 1848: "The lack of all real activity, all initiative, all independent intervention, the slowness of its own movements even in important areas, as for example the consideration of the constitutional recommendation, immediately demonstrated to the independent observer that the dominant elements were no longer in the chamber, but fought each other outside it." This state of parliamentary impotence, Stein argues, proves that "pure democracy and absolute democratic forms" were finished in France; democracy "was powerless, and still is" because the first principle of democracy is majority rule—but "the weakness of democracy lay in the fact that its own principles [such as majority rule] forced it to serve interests that would eliminate democracy's foundation, equality." See Lorenz von Stein, "Die socialistischen und communistischen Bewegungen seit der dritten französischen Revolution," Appendix in Stein's *Socialismus und Communismus des heutigen Frankreichs* (Leipzig: Wigand, 1848), 25–26. This issue was a persistent theme in Schmitt's work during the Republic; cf. "Legalität und gleiche Chance politischer Machtgewinnung," in *Legalität und Legitimität*. —tr.]

18. Charles Maurras, *L'avenir de l'intelligence* (Paris: Albert Fontemong, 1905, 2d edition), 98.

19. [Tr.] The Holy Alliance was formed in 1815 as a defense against democratic and revolutionary political movements in Europe after the French Revolution. It was based on a charter of substantial political goals and a shared identity among member states as Christian powers. By contrast the League of Nations had no such identity, as Schmitt's remark notes.

20. [Tr.] Cf. Carl Schmitt, *Die Kernfrage des Völkerbundes* (Berlin: Ferdinand Dümmler, 1926).

21. [Tr.] Cf. Schmitt's *Politische Theologie* (Munich & Leipzig: Duncker & Humblot, 1922).

2 The Principles of Parliamentarism

1. Egon Zweig, *Die Lehre vom pouvoir constituant* (Tübingen: Mohr, 1909).

2. [Tr] Monarchists in the French National Assembly argued that a single man could be the representative of the people. Cf. Karl Löwenstein, *Volk und Parlament nach der Staatstheorie der französischen Nationalversammlung von 1789* (Munich: Drei Masken Verlag, 1922).

3. Rudolf Smend, "Die Verschiebung der konstitutionellen Ordnung durch Verhältniswahl," in *Festgabe für Karl Bergbohm* [vol. 2] (Bonn: A. Marcus & E. Webers, 1919),
278; and Smend, "Die politische Gewalt im Verfassungsstaat und das Problem der
Staatsform," in *Festgabe für Wilhelm Kahl* (Tübingen: Mohr, 1923), 22. [Both are reprinted
in Smend, *Staatsrechtliche Abhandlungen* (Berlin: Duncker & Humblot, 1955, 1968), 60–88.
—tr.]

4. As characteristic of this view the following can be mentioned: Adhémar Esmein,
Éléments de droit constitutionnel (Paris: Librairie de la Société du Recueil Général des Lois
et des Arrets, 1909, 5th edition), 274: "Because the representative regime [by this he
means parliamentarism] is essentially a regime of debate and free discussion." Further,
in the seventh edition of the same work (Esmein-Nezard, 1921), vol. 1, 448, he explains
all the institutions of parliamentary constitutional law today by noting that such a
system "assumes the maximum liberty of decision and discussion in the legislative
assembly." See also Harold Laski, *The Foundations of Sovereignty* [New York: Harcourt,
Brace & Co., 1921], 36: "The fundamental hypothesis of government in a representative
system is that it is government by discussion."

5. Guizot, *Histoire des origines du gouvernement représentatif en France*, vol. 2 (Paris: Didier,
1851), 14. This book arose from lectures that Guizot held from 1820 onward and often
rewrote; it is the result of what an important scholar, an experienced politician, and
an honorable man observed and thought in the years from 1814 to 1848. His theory
of parliamentarism, inspired by the Anglo-Saxon spirit, Guizot called in the foreword
(dated May 1851) "the faith and hope that have filled my life and which until lately
have been the faith and hope of our times." The typical meaning of Guizot is well
recognized by Hugo Krabbe, *Die moderne Staatsidee* (The Hague: Martinus Nijhof, 1919),
178. Because of its exhaustive summary, Krabbe cites Guizot's opinion of parliamentarism
in full: "That is in addition the character of a system that nowhere acknowledges the
legitimacy of absolute power to oblige all citizens constantly and without restriction to
seek truth, reason, and justice, which have to check actual power. It is this which
constitutes the representative system: (1)through discussion the powers-that-be are obliged
to seek truth in common; (2) through publicity the powers are brought to this search
under the eyes of the citizenry; (3) through freedom of the press the citizens themselves
are brought to look for truth and to tell this to the powers-that-be." In the phrase
representative system, *representative* refers to the representation of the (rational) people in
parliament. The equation of parliamentarism and the representative system is characteristic of the confusion of the nineteenth century. The concept of representation has
a deeper problematic that has not yet been fully recognized. For my purposes here it
is enough to refer to parliamentarism and only briefly indicate the particular character
of the true concept of representation: It belongs essentially to the sphere of publicity
(in contrast to deputization, commission, mandate, and so forth, which are originally
concepts of civil law), and it assumes a personal worth in the persons representing and
represented and also in that person before whom representation is made (in contrast
to the representation of interests or management). To give a very clear example: In
the eighteenth century a prince was represented before other princes by his ambassador
(who must also be a nobleman), whereas economic and other sorts of business could
be left to "agents." In the struggle of parliament with absolute monarchy, parliament
appeared as the representative of the people (conceived as a unity). Where the people

were represented, the king could preserve his worth only as the representative of the people (as in the French constitution of 1791). Where absolute monarchy asserted itself, it had to contest the possibility or even the admissibility of popular representation and tried for that reason to make parliament into a body for the representation of corporate interests (as, for example, in Germany during 1815-1848). When a "free" in contrast to an "imperative" mandate is identified as the particular characteristic of a "representative" assembly, then this is explicable in terms of a practically important peculiarity. In truth parliament is not the representative of the whole people simply because it is dependent on the voters, for the voters are not the whole people. Only gradually in the course of the nineteenth century, as one could no longer imagine the concept of a person and it became something objective, did one confuse the sum of current voters (or their majority) for the overriding total person of the people or nation, and thus one lost the sense of the representation of the people and of representation altogether. In the struggle for representation in Germany during 1815-1848, this confusion is already indescribable; and it can scarcely be determined whether parliament should represent the people before the king (so that two are represented in the state, the king and the people), or whether parliament in addition to the king is a representative of the nation (for instance in France, where according to the constitution of 1791 there were two representatives). The historical description of the French National Assembly of 1789 and of the German struggle for a "representative constitution" suffers from the misunderstanding of a concept so important as representation. That is true even of a book that is as valuable and as important as Karl Löwenstein, *Volk und Parlament nach der Staatstheorie der französischen Nationalversammlung von 1789* (Munich, 1922) On the concept of representation in German literature between 1815 and 1848, see Emil Gerber's Bonn dissertation, 1926.

6. Robert von Mohl, *Staatsrecht, Völkerrecht und Politik. Monographien* vol. 1 (Tübingen: Verlag der H. Laupp'schen Buchhandlung, 1860-62), 5.

7. [Tr.] See Schmitt, *Politische Romantik* (Munich & Leipzig: Duncker & Humblot, 1919).

8. Wilhelm von Hasbach, *Die moderne Demokratie* (Jena: Gustav Fischer, 1913, 1921), and *Die parlamentarische Kabinettsregierung* (1919); see also Hasbach's article "Gewaltenteilung, Gewaltentrennung und gemischte Staatsform," *Vierteljahrsschrift für Sozial und Wirtschaftsgeschichte*, 13 (1916), 562.

9. Ferdinand Tönnies, *Kritik der öffentliche Meinung* (1922), 100.

10. There is more on this in my book on dictatorship, *Die Diktatur* (1921), 14ff.; see also Friedrich Meinecke, *Die Idee der Staatsräson* (Munich & Berlin: Oldenburg, 1924), and my review in the *Archiv für Sozialwissenschaft und Sozialpolitik*, 56 (1926), 226-234. [Schmitt refers here to Arnold Clapmar, *De Arcanis rerum publicarum* (Bremen, 1605). Schmitt's review of Meinecke was reprinted in Schmitt's *Positionen und Begriffe im Kampf mit Weimar, Genf, Versailles, 1923-39* (Hamburg: Hanseatische Verlag, 1940). Meinecke's *Staatsräson* has been translated as *Machiavellism: The Doctrine of Raison d'Etat and Its Place in Modern History* (London: Routledge, Kegan Paul, 1957). —tr.]

11. [Tr.] On the Monarchomachians see Harold Laski's introduction to the English translation of the *Vindiciae contra Tyrannos* of Junius Brutus: *A Defence of Liberty against*

Tyrants (London: G. Bell & Sons, 1924). Laski comments that "at the bottom of [the Monarchomachians'] argument is an emphasis which no political philosophy can afford to neglect. In part it is the realisation that every state is built upon the consciences of men. . . . In part also it is the insistence that the state exists to secure for its members some agreed minimum of civilization" (55). The Monarchomachian tradition originated in the massacre of Huguenots ordered by the Catholic monarch Catherine de Medici in September 1572; some two thousand French Protestants were murdered, and there followed a period of retaliation in other European countries in which Catholics were persecuted by Protestant monarchs, and Catholics by Protestants. On the Monarchomachians see also Albert Elkan, *Die Publizistik der Bartholomausnacht* (Heidelberg: Carl Winter, 1904), and Otto von Gierke, *Johannes Althusius und die Entwicklung der naturrechtlichen Staatstheorien* (Breslau, 1878), 3-4. Gierke's work has been translated as *The Development of Political Theory* (London: Allen & Unwin, 1939). Laski—and Schmitt here too—contrasts the *Vindiciae contra Tyrannos* with Bodin's *Les six livres de la République* (1576) as a text that upholds the concept of limited power against the unlimited sovereignty of absolute monarchs: he comments that in the late sixteenth century "Bodin was the innovator" while the *Vindiciae* upheld a medieval concept of the world governed by natural law (Laski, introduction to the *Vindiciae*, 47).

12. [Tr.] Economist and follower of François Quesnay, founder of the physiocrats, Le Mercier de la Rivière was counselor to Parlement before the revolution. In the years before the revolution he produced a series of tracts justifying the French monarch, and his most famous work, *L'Ordre naturel* (1767), justified the rights and property of the monarchy. He remained unrepentant throughout the Terror, and he died, persecuted, in 1793 or 1794. Cf. Lotte Silberstein, *Le Mercier de la Rivière und seine politischen Ideen* (Berlin: Emil Ebering, 1928).

13. Marquis de Condorcet in the "Discours sur les conventions nationales" (April 1, 1791) and also in the speech on monarchy and the republic (also 1791), in *Oeuvres*, vol. 11. The belief in the art of printing books is one of the characteristic signs of the revolutionary Enlightenment. An article from year one of the Republic, cited according to the *Citateur Republicain* (Paris, 1834), 97, enumerates the consequences: Every unfreedom, every burden, every obstacle to the general happiness will disappear, wars will cease and in their place wealth and surplus and virtue will appear—"such will be the benefits of printing."

14. Cf. Erich Kaufmann, *Kritik der neukantischen Rechtsphilosophie* (Tübingen: Mohr, 1921), 60-61.

15. In his work "On the Liberty of the Press and Public Discussion" (1821). [In *The Works of Jeremy Bentham*, ed. John Bowring, vol. 2 (Edinburgh: Tait, 1843), 275-297. — tr.]

16. [Tr.] J. S. Mill, *On Liberty* (1859).

17. Maurice Hauriou, *Précis de droit administratif et de droit public* (Paris, 1914); Redslob, *Die parlamentarische Regierung* (1918).

18. Rousseau talks about a balance of interests in the general will; cf. *Du contrat social*, Bk. II, chap. 9, sect. 4; Bk. II, chap. 11, note; Bk. II, chap. 6, sect. 10; Bk. III, chap. 8, sect. 10; Bk. IV, chap. 4, sect. 25; Bk. V; see esp. Bk. I, chap. 8, sect. 2; Bk. II, chap. 6, sect. 10; Bk. III, chap. 8, sect. 10.

19. [Tr.] Montesquieu, *L'Esprit des lois* (1748); translated as *The Spirit of the Laws* (Chicago: Encyclopedia Britannica, 1952). On Montesquieu's political thought see the aptly named chapter "The British Constitution," in Kingsley Martin, *French Liberal Thought in the Eighteenth Century* (London: Phoenix, 1962), 147ff.

20. [Tr.] John Locke, *Two Treatises of Government* (1690), Second Treatise, sect. 172.

21. [Tr.] Cf. Thomas Hobbes, *Behemoth; or, The Long Parliament* (1679); a modern edition was prepared by Ferdinand Tönnies (Cambridge: Cambridge University Press, 1889). On the Long Parliament and the English Civil War see Christopher Hill, *The Intellectual Origins of the English Revolution* (Oxford: Clarendon Press, 1965), and *God's Englishman: Oliver Cromwell and the English Revolution* (London: Weidenfeld & Nicholson, 1970).

22. [Tr.] Cf. Martin, *French Liberal Thought in the Eighteenth Century*, and "Acte constitutionnel du 24 Juin 1793, et Declaration des droit de l'homme et du citoyen," in Léon Duguit and Henry Monnier, *Les Constitutions et les principales lois politiques de la France depuis 1789* (Paris: Librairie Générale de Droit et de Jurisprudence, 1915, 3d edition).

23. Cf. my book *Die Diktatur* (1921), 149.

24. Theodore de Beza, *Droit de Magistrats* (1574). ["The theory of Calvinist politics is here set forth with perfect clarity. To God alone does absolute power belong. Magistrates indeed have wide authority and they cannot be held to account by the people . . . but when the tyranny becomes intolerable, just remedies must be used against it. Not, however, by every member of the state. The ordinary citizen is bound by the conditions of his citizenship to submit. . . . There are, however, in each state a body of citizens whose function it is to see that the sovereign does his duty; in France the States-General is such a body of such men. . . . Royalty is, even though divine in nature, essentially dependent upon popular institution" (Laski, introduction to *Vindiciae contra Tyrannos*, 24–25). Beza's pamphlet was the first during the civil wars to assert the principle of popular sovereignty, and according to Laski, Beza can be considered the first Monarchomachian. —tr.]

25. Junius Brutus, *Vindiciae contra Tyrannos*. [Schmitt refers to pages 115–116 of an Edinburgh edition of 1579. See the English translation introduced by Laski (note 11). —tr.]

26. Grotius, *De jure belli ac Pacis*, Bk. I, chap. 3, sect. 6 (Amsterdam, 1631). Grotius also uses the comparison with mathematics in order to justify his negative estimation of particular facts.

27. [Tr.] Otto Mayer, *Deutsches Verwaltungsrecht* (Munich & Leipzig: Duncker & Humblot, 1895–96).

28. Erich Kaufmann's exposition of Locke in his *Untersuchungsausschluss und Staatsgerichthof* (Berlin: G. Stelka, 1920) is a perfect example of Locke's immediate and practical relevance today. Kaufmann's work must also be noted because of its importance for the material concept of law (*materielle Gesetzesbegriff*).

29. John Neville Figgis, *The Divine Right of Kings* (Cambridge: Cambridge University Press, 1914, 2d edition).

30. John Marshall's opinion appears as the motto of chapter 16 in James Beck's book on the American constitution. [Schmitt refers to the German translation of Beck, *The American Constitution* (Oxford: Oxford University Press, 1924), which appeared as *Die Verfassung der Vereinigten Staaten von Amerika* (Berlin: Walter de Gruyter, 1926). A foreword by Calvin Coolidge and an introduction by Walter Simons, interim president of the Weimar Republic and later chief justice of the German Supreme Court, appeared in the German edition. Chief Justice John Marshall established the principle of judicial review in the American constitution. In the last years of the Weimar Republic, Schmitt was involved in a debate with Hans Kelsen and others on the question of a "defender of the constitution." While Kelsen argued that judicial review would be the best solution to the question of which of the republic's governmental branches should be the authoritative interpreter of the constitution and thus its "defender," Schmitt, after briefly sharing this point of view, argued in *Der Hüter der Verfassung* (1931) that the Reichspräsident was best suited to defend the constitution. Cf. the 1931 version of this discussion with Schmitt's "Der Hüter der Verfassung," *Archiv des öffentlichen Rechts*, 16 (1929), 161–237. See also Bendersky, *Carl Schmitt: Theorist for the Reich* (Princeton: Princeton University Press, 1983), 112ff., and Ellen Kennedy, "Bendersky, *Carl Schmitt: Theorist for the Reich*," *History of Political Thought*, 4 (1983), 582ff.; see also George Schwab, *The Challenge of the Exception* (Berlin: Duncker & Humblot, 1970), 80ff. —tr.]

31. *Politische Theologie*, 4ff. [Schmitt defines the sovereign as whoever decides the question of a state of exception ("Souverän ist, wer über den Ausnahmezustand entscheidet"). Cf. Pufendorf's discussion in *De jure naturae* (Bk. VII, chap. 6, sect. 8), quoted above. On Bodin see Julian H. Franklin's study, *Jean Bodin and the Rise of Absolutist Theory* (Cambridge: Cambridge University Press, 1973). —tr.]

32. [Tr.] Paul Laband was one of the founders of legal positivism in Germany. See Peter Oertzen, *Die soziale Funktion des staatsrechtlichen Postivismus* (Frankfurt: Suhrkamp Verlag, 1974), and Walter Wilhelm, *Zur juristischen Methodenlehre im 19. Jahrhundert. Die Herkunft der Methode Paul Labands aus der Privatrechtlichenwissenschaft* (Frankfurt: Klostermann, 1958).

33. *Leviathan*, chap. 26, p. 137 of the English edition of 1651. [Schmitt refers to the chapter "Of Civil Laws," in Hobbes, *Leviathan*, ed. Michael Oakeshott (Oxford: Blackwells, 1946). —tr.]

34. *Dissertation on Parties*, letter 10.

35. On this see the extremely interesting examination by Joseph Barthélemy, *Le rôle du pouvoir exécutif dans les republiques modernes* (Paris: Giard & Briere, 1906), 489. The

citation above is taken from Condorcet's "Rapport sur le projet girondin," in *Archives parlementaires*, vol. 58, 583 (quoted by Barthélemy).

36. Titre VII, sect. II, art. 3, in "contrast" to laws the characteristic of decrees are "local or particular application, and the necessity of their being renewed after a certain period." The constitution of June 21, 1793 (articles 54 and 55), defined the concept of law in the usual way, according to subject matter. Leon Duguit and Henry Monnier, *Les Constitutions et les principales lois politiques de la France depuis 1789* (1915), 52.

37. G. W. F. Hegel, *Enzyklopädie*, sect. 544. [There were three editions of Hegel's *Enzyklopädie*; this paragraph does not appear in the first one (1817) but was included in Karl Rosenkranz's edition (Berlin: L. Heimann, 1870). The paragraph continues with a critical discussion of the concept of a check on government through the budget law. It concludes by rejecting the theory of balance of powers within the state as "a contradiction of the fundamental idea of what a state is" (449). —tr.]

38. Ernst Zitelmann, *Irrtum und Rechtsgeschäft* (Leipzig: Duncker & Humblot, 1879).

39. [Tr.] Duguit and Monnier, *Les Constitutions*, 260.

40. Alexander Hamilton, *The Federalist Papers*, No. 70 (March 18, 1788). Montesquieu (*L'Esprit des lois*, Bk. XI, chap. 6) is also of the opinion that the executive must be in the hands of a single person because it requires immediate action; legislation by contrast can often better (as he cautiously puts it) be decided by many rather than by one man. On popular representation Montesquieu makes the characteristic remark that the great advantage of the representatives is that they "are able to discuss affairs. The people are not at all capable of that; and that is one of the great inconveniences of democracy." The distinction between legislation as advice and reflection and execution as action can be found again in Sieyès. Cf. his *Politische Schriften* (1796), vol. 2, 384.

41. That deism maintains that God is an otherworldly authority is of great importance for the conception of a balance of powers. It makes a difference whether a third person holds the balance or the balance derives from counterbalancing forces. Swift's remark in 1701 is typical of the first conception of balance (and important for Bolingbroke's theory of balance): "The 'balance of power' supposes three things: first, the part which is held, together with the hand that holds it; and then the two scales with whatever is weighed therein." I am grateful to Eduard Rosenbaum for calling my attention to this citation; cf. also *Weltwirtschaftliches Archiv*, 18 (1922), 423. [Schmitt's citation of Swift is taken from Eduard Rosenbaum's article "Eine Geschichte der Pariser Friedenskonferenz," which was a review of H. W. V. Temperley's *A History of the Peace Conference of Paris*, 5 vols. (London: Henry Frouda, Hodder & Stoughton, 1920–21). —tr.]

42. Condorcet, *Oeuvres*, vol. 13, 18.

43. [Tr.] Cf. Schmitt, *Politische Romantik* (1919).

44. G. W. F. Hegel, *Rechtsphilosophie* (1821), sects. 301, 314, 315, and see sects. 315 and 316 for the citations which follow in the text. [English citations are taken from T. M.

Knox's translation, *Hegel's Philosophy of Right* (Oxford: Oxford University Press, 1973). —tr.]

45. Robert von Mohl, *Enzyklopädie der Staatswissenschaft* (Tübingen: Laupp'schen Buchhandlung, 1872), 655.

46. J. C. Bluntschli, "Parteien, politische," in Bluntschli and K. Brater, eds., *Deutsches-Staatswörterbuch*, vol. 7 (Stuttgart & Leipzig: Expedition des Staatswörterbuches, 1861), 717–747. On Lorenz von Stein see my *Politische Theologie*, 53. This explanation of the parties, which is characteristic for German liberalism, is also found in Friedrich Meinecke, *Staatsräson*, 525. [Schmitt's citation is inaccurate; the discussion of political parties is on pages 537–538. Meinecke argues here that political parties belong to the healthy political life of the state just as contradictions and pluralism belong to individual life. Although the argument appears characteristically liberal at this stage, Meinecke later notes that "parliamentarism only temporarily fills the statesman with Staatsräson; his attention soon turns to the next election" (538). —tr.]

47. J. K. Bluntschli, *Allgemeines Staatsrecht* (Stuttgart: J. G. Cotta'schen Buchhandlung, 1876, 5th edition). An interesting combination of the good old understanding of the principles of parliamentarism and modern misunderstandings is the article by Adolf Neumann-Hofer, "Die Wirksamkeit der Kommissionen in den Parlamenten," *Zeitschrift für Politik*, 4 (1911), 51ff. He starts from the assumption that experience has shown that public discussion no longer takes place in popular assemblies, but he believes that in order to preserve discussion, the committees could become "discussion clubs" (64–65). On the misunderstanding of the concept of discussion here, see the preface, above. [On Robert von Mohl's argument for parliamentarism see his *Representativsystem* (1860), discussed in James J. Sheehan, *German Liberalism in the Nineteenth Century* (London: Methuen, 1982), 116, 385. —tr.]

48. [Tr.] Locke, *Two Treatises*, Second Treatise, sect. 172.

49. Eugene Forçade, *Études historiques* (Paris: Michel Levy, 1853), in a review of Lamartine's history of the revolution of 1848. Lamartine is also an example of the belief in discussion, which he contrasts with power and force. Both his *Sur la Politique Rationelle* (1831) and *Le Passé, le Présent, l'Avanir de la Republique* (1848) are inspired by this. He even thinks that the newspapers appear in the morning like a rising sun that dispels darkness! Victor Hugo's poetic description of the *Tribune* in his famous *Napoléon le Petit* is absolutely characteristic and of great importance as a symptom. The belief in discussion characterizes this epoch. Thus Hauriou, *Précis de droit constitutionnel* (Paris: Recueil Sirey, 1923), 198, 201, describes the age of parliamentarism as the age of discussion ("l'âge de la discussion"), and a staunch liberal such as Yves Guyot contrasts parliamentary government resting on discussion (for him, of course, a "gouvernement de discussion") with the "atavism" of all politics that does not rest on discussion. Guyot, *Politique Parlamentaire—Politique Atavique* (Paris, Felix Alcan, 1924). In this way parliamentarism becomes identical with freedom and culture altogether. L. Gumplowicz completely dissolves all these concepts: "The character and peculiarity of Asiatic culture is despotism; [that of] European culture, the parliamentary regime." Ludwig Gumplowicz, *Soziologie und Politik* (Leipzig: Duncker

& Humblot, 1892), 116. [Schmitt refers to Alphonse Lamartine, *Histoire de la Revolution de 1848* (Paris: Penotin, 1848). —tr.]

3 Dictatorship in Marxist Thought

1. [Tr.] The July revolution in Paris (1830) led to the abdication of Charles X. Louis-Philippe, the Citizen King, succeeded him and inaugurated "the golden age of the bourgeoisie." Eighteen years later the February revolution in Paris led to Louis-Philippe's own abdication and the establishment of a French republic under Louis-Napoleon, the nephew of Napoleon Bonapart. In the same year (1848) Marx and Engels published *The Communist Manifesto* and Europe's conservative order was shaken by a series of riots and revolutions. A socialist uprising in June was brutally repressed by the authorities in Paris and it is to this conflict of class interest between the bourgeoisie on one side and the peasants and workers on the other that Schmitt refers when he says that "in opposition to parliamentary constitutionalism, not to democracy, the idea of a dictatorship that would sweep away parliamentarism regained its topicality." Cf. Karl Marx, "The Class Struggles in France, 1848–1850," Marx and Engels, *Selected Works*, vol. 1 (Moscow: Progress Publishers, 1977), 186–299.

2. In this alliance during the nineteenth century—as once in the alliance with the church—philosophy played only a modest role; but nonetheless it cannot so soon renounce the alliance. Further, H. Pichler, *Zur Philosophie der Geschichte* (Tübingen: Mohr, 1922), 16.

3. [Tr.] Schmitt refers to the utopian socialist Ernst Bloch, whom he knew in Munich. Of Bloch's works perhaps the most relevant to this point is *Geist der Utopie* (Munich: Duncker & Humblot, 1918); a second, enlarged edition appeared in 1923 (Berlin: Paul Cassirer, 1923). See further Bloch's *Freiheit und Ordnung. Abriss der Sozialutopien* (Berlin, Aufbau Verlag, 1947).

4. [Tr.] Cf. Shirley Letwin, *The Pursuit of Certainty: Hume, Bentham, Mill, Beatrice Webb* (Cambridge: Cambridge University Press, 1965). See also F. A. Hayek, *The Road to Serfdom* (London: Routledge, Kegan Paul, 1977), originally published in 1944, and Hayek's essay "*The Road to Serfdom* after Twelve Years" (1956), in his *Studies in Philosophy, Politics, and Economics* (London: Routledge, Kegan Paul, 1967). These texts by contemporary "classical liberals" reveal a fascinating connection between their views of the Enlightenment and Schmitt's, despite Hayek's vigorous criticism of the former in *The Road to Serfdom*. F. R. Cristi has explored the relationship between Schmitt and Hayek in "Hayek and Schmitt on the Rule of Law," *Canadian Journal of Political Science* 17:3 (1984), 521–535.

5. [Tr.] "Die Weltgeschichte ist auch das Weltgericht," a phrase usually associated with Hegel, was taken from Friedrich Schiller's poem "Resignation." Schiller, *Werke* (Berlin & Leipzig: Deutsches Verlagshaus Bong & Co., n.d.). See also Hegel, *Grundlinien der Philosophie des Rechts* (1821), para. 340, and the *Enzyklopädie* (1817), para. 448.

6. [Tr.] Cf. Hegel, *Geschichte der Philosophie*, III: "Fichte never achieves the Idea of Reason, as the complete real unity of Subject and Object, of Ego and non-Ego. For him it is merely an ought, an aim." Quoted in J. N. Findley, *The Philosophy of Hegel* (New York: Collier Books, 1966), 49.

7. [Tr.] The Battle of Jena, in which Napoleon defeated the combined forces of Russia and Prussia, was fought as Hegel completed the *Phänomenologie des Geistes* (1807). Historians usually date the end of the Holy Roman Empire of the German Nation from 1806. f. also Hegel, "The German Constitution" (1799–1802), in J. Pelczynski, ed., *Hegel's Political Writings* (Oxford: Clarendon Press, 1964). On October 13, 1806, Hegel wrote in a letter, "I saw Napoleon, the soul of the world, riding through the town on a reconnaissance. It is indeed wonderful to see, concentrated in a point, sitting on a horse, an individual who overruns the world and masters it." Quoted in Pelczynski (7).

8. [Tr.] On the young Hegelians see Charles Taylor, *Hegel* (Cambridge: Cambridge University Press, 1975).

9. [Tr.] Much French art and literature of the nineteenth century depicts the bourgeois as a figure of ridicule and spite. See for example Gustave Flaubert's *Bouvard et Pécuchet* (1881). Henry James's comment in *Daumier, Caricaturist* sums up the social content of Daumier's drawings: "He has no wide horizon; the absolute bourgeois hems him in, and he is a bourgeois himself without poetic ironies, to whom a big cracked mirror is given." See also T. J. Clark, *The Absolute Bourgeois: Artists and Politics in France, 1848–1851* (London: Thames & Hudson, 1973).

10. [Tr.] Karl Marx and Friedrich Engels, *The Communist Manifesto* (1848), in Marx and Engels, *Selected Works*, 108–137; Karl Marx, *Das Kapital* (1867–94), translated as *Capital* (Moscow: Progress Publishers, 1965). Marx had already identified the fundamental contradiction of David Ricardo's "bourgeois classical political economy" as the relationship between the purchase and sale of labor and its value. "The Ricardian school," Engels comments, "was wrecked mainly by the insolubility of this contradiction. Classical economics had got into a blind alley. The man who found the way out of this blind alley was Karl Marx." Engels, Introduction to Karl Marx, "Wage Labour and Capital" (1849), in Marx and Engels, *Selected Works*, vol. 7, 146.

11. [Tr.] "Ricardo is the chief and last development of bourgeois political economy, which has made no progress since him. He developed the bourgeois economy to its epitome, that is, to its depths where nothing else was left to its theory but to transform itself into social-economy." Ferdinand Lassalle, "Herr Bastiat Schulze v. Delitsch: Der Ökonomische Julian, oder Kapital und Arbeit" (1864), in *Gesammelte Reden und Schriften*, ed. E. Bernstein, vol. 5 (Berlin: Cassier, 1919), 216–217. Lassalle comments further in this chapter ("Tausch, Wert und Freie Konkurrenz") that "social democracy today fights against you (Schulze-Delitsch) instead of Ricardo. This only shows how degenerate the European bourgeoisie has become." Schulze-Delitsch was a liberal parliamentarian who became convinced that "the way to reform was to be found in social and economic rather than political life." He organized the cooperative movement in Germany and hoped that it would provide a way to achieve social reform within a free economy.

See James J. Sheehan, *German Liberalism in the Nineteenth Century* (London: Methuen, 1982), 92.

12. [Tr.] Hegel, *Phänomenologie des Geistes* (1807), cited according to the English translation by James Baillie, *The Phenomenology of Mind* (London: George Allen & Unwin, 1910), 366.

13. This is not merely a figure of speech. If a social nonentity is possible in society, then it proves specifically that no social order exists. There can be no social order that contains such a vacuum.

14. [Tr.] The importance of England as a model of capitalist development and bourgeois society for Marx's theory can hardly be exaggerated, and it is neatly summed up by Engels's answer in his *Principles of Communism* (1847) to the question, "How did the proletariat arise?": "The Proletariat arose as a result of the industrial revolution which unfolded in England in the latter half of the last (i.e., eighteenth) century and which has repeated itself since then in all the civilized countries of the world" (Marx and Engels, *Selected Works*, 81). Cf. Michael Evans, *Karl Marx* (London: George Allen & Unwin, 1976).

15. Condorcet's *Tableau historique* (1794) refutes Rousseau's thesis in *Discours sur les arts et sciences* (1750) that knowledge and cultivation of the arts and science had led to the degeneration of morals. In Condorcet's view, progress is identical with knowledge and the struggle against superstition, priests, and error. Significantly, he identifies the discovery of printing as the instrument that created a new tribunal of public opinion. In the last epoch, Condorcet asked, could there not come a time when the well-being of the populace would start to deteriorate, and when in contrast to the steady progress of all previous ages there would be "a retrograde movement, at least a kind of movement between good and evil" beyond which no further improvement is possible? Kingsley Martin, *French Liberal Thought in the Eighteenth Century* (London: Phoenix, 1962), 281ff.

16. [Tr.] In a conversation on May 12, 1982, Carl Schmitt emphasized the importance of this last sentence for his understanding of contemporary politics and for the appreciation of the dilemma he sought to clarify in this text. The liberal "system" is a dialectic, but it only allows dictatorship in the form of education; this alone breaks into its discussion. For Hegel, dialectics were a means for the analysis of society, but Marx transforms this *Gesellschatsanalyse* into *Klassenkampf*. This struggle needs no education; rather it is a war in which the enemy will be destroyed ("ein Krieg in dem die Feinde vernichtet werden"). This transforms Hegelian philosophy into a political theology. About the last sentence of this chapter Schmitt commented, "It is a matter of life and death. Marx understood his enemy—the bourgeois liberal—better than he understood himself." Schmitt went on to quote Bruno Bauer: "Only the man who knows his prey better than it knows itself can trap it." Cf. Carl Schmitt, "Die legale Weltrevolution: Politischer Mehrwert als Prämie auf juristische Legalität und Superlegalität," *Der Staat*, 3 (1978), 321–339.

4 Irrationalist Theories of the Direct Use of Force

1. [Tr.] Isaac Deutscher provides a vivid description of the Bolshevists in the October revolution in *The Prophet Armed: Trotsky, 1879–1921* (Oxford: Oxford Unversity Press, 1970); on Cromwell and the Levellers see Christopher Hill, *God's Englishman* (London: Weidenfeld & Nicholson, 1970).

2. [Tr.] Engels in *Anti-Dühring* (1877–78) already suggests a "dictatorship of the proletariat," but Lenin gave the idea its definitive practical statement. See V. I. Lenin, *Lenin's Theses on Bourgeois Democracy and Proletarian Dictatorship* (Glasgow: Socialist Labour Press, 1920). The relationship between art and politics in the Soviet Union's first years was much more complicated than Schmitt's reference to a *Proletkult* allows, but there was nevertheless a deliberate mesh of the two in the years after the revolution. Alexander Rodschenko and Warwara Stepanowa's *Producer's Manifesto* (Moscow, 1921) gives some indication of the tone and political content of contemporary Soviet art: "The task of the Constructivist group is to give a communist expression to material, constructive work." The manifesto continues with an affirmation of communism based on historical materialism as the only basis for science and concludes with the slogans of the constructivists, among them: "Down with art, long live technique." Cited according to the text in *Tendenzen der Zwanziger Jahre, 15. Europäische Kunstaustellung, Berlin, 1977* (Berlin: Dietrich Reimer Verlag, 1977), 102–103. But Schmitt seems to refer here to the increased preoccupation of art in the 1920s with the lives and surroundings of workers and objects from the everyday world of the working class. The 1977 Berlin catalogue is an excellent source of images characteristic of this tendency, but see also David Mellor's *Germany: The New Photography, 1927–33* (London: Arts Council of Great Britain Publications, 1978) for the development and adaptation of the art of proletarian culture in Germany.

3. [Tr.] Enrico Ferri appears in Michels's *Sociologie des Parteiwesens in der modernen Demokratie* (Leipzig: Alfred Kronen Verlag, 1926) and *Storia critica del Movimento Socialista Italiano* (Florence: Societa an Editrice "La Voce," 1926) as an example of the new type of political leader. A professor of law, Ferri became the leader of the Italian Socialist party in 1893; after 1922 he joined the Fascists and was made a senator by Mussolini. He was the author of an influential study of positivism: *Socialismo e scienza positivista: Darwin, Spencer, Marx* (1894) and a definitive text on criminal law, *Sociologia Criminale* (1900). Ferri's *Die revolutionäre Methode* (Leipzig: Hirschfeld, 1907–10) was translated with an introduction by Michels.

4. Georges Sorel, *Réflexions sur la violence* (Paris: Études sur le Devenir social, 1919); the fourth edition is cited here. Sorel's *Réflexions* was first published in 1906 in the journal *Mouvement socialist*. [English translation by T. E. Hulme with an introduction by Edward Shils, *Reflections on Violence* (New York: Collier Books, 1972). —tr.]

5. In Germany Sorel is still scarcely known today (1926), and while innumerable texts have been translated into German in recent years, Sorel has been ignored—perhaps because of the "endless conversation." Wyndham Lewis is perfectly correct to say that "Georges Sorel is the key to all contemporary political thought" (*The Art of Being Ruled*,

128). [H. Stuart Hughes, *The Obstructed Path: French Social Thought in the Years of Desperation* (New York: Harper & Row, 1968), discusses Sorel's importance for social thought in this century. On the connection between Sorel's political theory and Bergson's philosophy, see Ellen Kennedy, "Bergson's Philosophy and French Political Doctrines: Sorel, Maurras, Peguy, and de Gaulle," *Government and Opposition*, 15 (1980), 75–91. —tr.]

6. [Tr.] Cf. Benedetto Croce, *Materialismo storico ed economia marxista* (1900). Croce thought Karl Marx and Georges Sorel "the only original theorists of socialism." His Italian translation of the *Réflexions* was read by Mussolini, and after 1922 Croce became a leading Fascist philosopher.

7. *Politische Theologie*, 45.

8. Michael Bakunin, *Oeuvres*, vol. 4 (Paris: Stock, 1911), 428 (on the exchange with Marx during 1872), and vol. 2, 34–42 (on referenda as the new lie).

9. Fritz Brupbacher, *Marx und Bakunin: Ein Beitrag zur Geschichte der internationalen Arbeiterassoziation* (Munich: Birk, 1913), 74ff. [There is a discussion of Bakunin and Bergson on pages 75–76 of Brupbacher's book. See also J. J. Hamilton, "Georges Sorel and the Inconsistencies of a Bergsonian Marxism," *Political Theory*, 1 (1973), 329–340. Bergson's *L'Évolution créatrice* (1907) interpreted history in terms of a knowing creator. His work as a whole grew out of a critique of science and positivism and at the heart of Bergson's philosophy there is an assertion that God (however conceived) is more important than the cold calculations of modern science. This is finally the meaning of *élan vital* in Bergsonian thought. Bergson, *Creative Evolution*, trans. D. Mitchell (New York: Holt, 1911). The literature on Bergson is enormous; a comprehensive bibliography up to 1974 is provided in P. A. Y. Gunter, *Henri Bergson: A Bibliography* (Bowling Green, Oh.: Philosophy Documentation Center, 1974). —tr.]

10. [Tr.] Cf. Sorel, *Réflexions*. For a contemporary statement of this view, see C. B. MacPherson, *The Life and Times of Liberal Democracy* (Oxford: Oxford University Press, 1977), in which liberal democracy is (according to the most consistent of MacPherson's definitions of it) "the democracy of a capitalist market society" in which liberalism means "the freedom of the stronger to do down the weaker by following market rules."

11. [Tr.] Proudhon, *La Guerre et la paix* (1861), in *Oeuvres completes*, vols. 13–14 (Paris: Librairie Internationale, 1867–70).

12. "Llegua el dia de las negaciones radicales o de las afirmaciones soberanas," *Obras*, vol. 4, 155 (in the essay "Catholicism, Liberalism, and Socialism"). Donoso-Cortés, *Obras de Don Juan Donoso-Cortés* (Madrid: Tejado, 1854–55), 10 vols. See also Carl Schmitt, *Donoso Cortés in gesamteuropäischer Interpretation* (Cologne: Greven Verlag, 1950).—tr.]

13. [Tr.] Charles-Forbes, Comte de Montalembert (1810–1870) represented Catholic liberalism in mid-nineteenth-century France. He opposed the Ultramontanes, engaging in a long controversy with their leader Louis Veuillot. He also resisted the doctrine of papal infallibility, but when reprimanded by the Curia, Montalembert submitted. He

was an immediate supporter of the February revolution of 1848 and fought for the separation of church and state in France.

14. [Tr.] Proudhon was "an ideologist of the petite bourgeoisie" for Marx. See Marx's "Letter to P. V. Annenkov in Paris" (December 28, 1846), in which he criticizes Proudhon's philosophy as "a phantasmagoria which presumptuously claims to be dialectical" and Proudhon himself as a man for whom "bourgeois life is an eternal verity." Marx and Engels, *Selected Works*, vol. 1 (Moscow: Progress Publishers, 1977), 519, 524.

15. To this comment in the first edition, I must today add the following: "the two actual opponents within the sphere of Western culture." Proudhon remained completely within an inherited moral tradition; the family based strictly on *pater potestas* and monogamy formed his ideal; that contradicted consequential anarchism. Cf. my *Politische Theologie* (1922), 5. The real enemy of all traditional concepts of West European culture appeared first with the Russians, particularly Bakunin. Proudhon and Sorel are both— Wyndham Lewis is right—still "Romans," not anarchists like the Russians (*The Art of Being Ruled*, 360). J. J. Rousseau, whom Wyndham Lewis also identifies as a true anarchist, does not seem to me to be a clear case because as a romantic his relation to the family and the state is only an example of romantic occasionalism. [Attacking Rousseau as a romantic was an especially popular theme of the Action Française in the years before 1914; see Kennedy, "Bergson's Philosophy and French Political Doctrines," 80–84. — tr.]

16. Sorel, *Réflexions*, 319.

17. [Tr.] The German war of liberation fought against the French occupying forces initiated "a genuine popular awakening," and the reforms of the Prussian minister Karl vom Stein "started from the fundamental idea of raising a moral, religious and patriotic spirit in the nation." See E. J. Passant, *Germany, 1815–1945* (Cambridge: Cambridge University Press, 1971), 6–7; also James J. Sheehan, *German Liberalism in the Nineteenth Century* (London: Methuen, 1982), 7ff.

18. Sorel, *Réflexions*, 372, 376.

19. [Tr.] Sorel replied to Eduard Bernstein in the *Réflexions*, 251: "la dictatur du proletariat . . . signaler un souvenir de l'Ancien Regime." Cf. Peter Gay, *The Dilemma of Democratic Socialism: Eduard Bernstein's Challenge to Marx* (New York: Columbia University Press, 1952).

20. Sorel, *Matériaux d'une théorie du prolétariat* (Paris: Marcel Rivière, 1919), 53. [See also notes 2 and 19, above. —tr.]

21. Sorel, *Réflexions*, 268.

22. One cannot object to the fact that Sorel relies on Bergson. His antipolitical (i.e., anti-intellectual) theory is based on a philosophy of concrete life, and such a philosophy has, like Hegelianism, a variety of practical applications. In France Bergson's philosophy has served the interests of a return to conservative tradition and Catholicism and, at the same time, radical, atheistic anarchism. That is by no means a sign of its falsehood.

The phenomenon has an interesting parallel in the conflict between right Hegelians and left Hegelians. One could say that philosophy has its own real life if it can bring into existence actual contradictions and organize battling opponents as living enemies. From this perspective it is remarkable that only the opponents of parliamentarism have drawn this vitality from Bergson's philosophy. By contrast German liberalism in the middle of the nineteenth century used the concept of life to support the parliamentary constitutional system and saw parliament as the living representative of social differences.

23. [Tr.] Sorel wrote an appendix to the fourth edition of the *Réflexions* entitled "Pour Lenine" (*Réflexions*, 437–454).

24. [Tr.] Patrick Pearse and James Connolly were executed by British firing squads after the Easter Rising (1916) was suppressed. Both became heroes of the Irish national movement, but Connolly's death took on an almost mystical importance in Irish politics partly because he was already so badly wounded that British troops had to tie him to a chair for the execution. Connolly's Marxist analysis has had little impact, but his death became a powerful symbol in Ireland's later political history. Pearse, it has been claimed, "has had more influence on the Ireland of the twentieth century than any other person." See P. MacAonghusa, *Quotations from P. H. Pearse* (Dublin & Cork: Mercier Press, 1979). Although the metaphors of their nationalism are different—Pearse's is a mystical Catholic nationalism, Connolly's is Marxism—they are both united by the definition of a mystique of death and national salvation that is still current in Irish politics today.

25. Trotsky at the Fourth World Congress of the Third International, on Freemasonry. [Cf. Deutscher, *The Prophet Armed.* —tr.]

26. [Tr.] Mussolini's speech in Naples, on October 24, 1922, was a landmark on the way to the Fascist takeover in Italy. See Adrian Lyttelton, *The Seizure of Power: Fascism in Italy, 1919–1929* (London: Weidenfeld & Nicholson, 1973).

27. [Tr.] Beyerle, *Parlamentarisches System—oder was sonst?* (Munich: Pfeiffer & Co., Verlag, 1921).

Bibliography to the 1926 Edition

Some of Schmitt's references are either incomplete or inaccurate. Wherever possible notes and bibliographical entries have been completed and corrected; but in some cases this was impossible, either because the edition he used was not available to me or the reference was too scant to allow Schmitt's source to be traced. The Bibliography is therefore somewhat inconsistent. Nevertheless, I hope that the reader will bear with this defect and find it a useful guide to the intellectual sources of this essay. (EK)

Bakunin, Michael, *Oeuvres*, 5 vols. Paris: Stock, 1911.

Barthélemy, Joseph, *Le rôle du pouvoir exécutif dans les republiques modernes*. Paris: Giard & Brière.

Beck, James M., *Die Verfassung der Vereinigten Staaten von Amerika*. Berlin: Walter de Gruyter, 1926. (German translation by Alfred Friedmann with a foreword by Calvin Coolidge and introduction by Walter Simons.)

Becker, Werner, "Demokratie und Massenstaat," *Die Schildgenossen* 5 (1924–25), 459–478.

Belloc, Hillaire, and Cecil Chesterton, *The Party System*. London: Stephen Swift, 1911.

Bentham, Jeremy, "On the Liberty of the Press and Public Discussion" (1821), in *The Works of Jeremy Bentham*, ed. John Bowring, vol. 2. Edinburgh: Tait, 1843, 275–297.

Berthélemy, Henry, *Traité élémentaire de droit administratif.* Paris: Rousseau, 1923 (10th edition).

Beyerle, Karl, *Parlamentarisches System—oder was sonst?* Munich: Pfeiffer & Co., Verlag, 1921.

Beza, Theodor de, *Droit des Magistrats.* 1574.

Bluntschli, Johann Kasper, "Parteien, politische," in Bluntschli and K. Brater, *Deutsches-Staatswörterbuch.* Stuttgart & Leipzig: Expedition des Staatswörterbuches, 1861.

Bluntschli, Johann Kasper, *Allgemeines Staatsrecht.* Stuttgart: J. G. Cotta'schen Buchhandlung, 1876 (5th edition).

Bolingbroke, Henry St. John, Viscount, "Dissertation on Parties." 1688.

Bonn, M. J., *Die Auflösung des modernen Staates.* Berlin: Verlag für Wirtschaft und Politik, 1921.

Bonn, M. J., *Die Krisis der europäischen Demokratie.* Tübingen: Mohr, 1925.

Bonn, M. J., and M. Palyi, *Die Wirtschaftswissenschaft nach dem Kriege. Festgabe für Lujo Brentano zum 80. Geburtstag.* Munich & Leipzig: Duncker & Humblot, 1925.

Bonner Festgabe für Ernst Zitelmann. Munich & Leipzig: Duncker & Humblot, 1923.

Brauweiler, Heinz, "Parlamentarismus und berufsständische Politik." *Preussische Jahrbücher,* 202 (1925), 58–72.

Brauweiler, Heinz. *Berufsstand und Staat.* Berlin: Ring Verlag, 1925.

Brinkmann, Carl, "Carl Schmitt's *Politische Romantik.*" *Archiv für Sozialwissenschaft und Sozialpolitik,* 54 (1925), 530–536.

Brupbacher, Fritz, *Marx und Bakunin: Ein Beitrag zur Geschichte der internationalen Arbeiterassoziation.* Munich: Birk, 1913.

Burckhardt, Jacob, *Briefe,* 5 vols., ed. Max Burckhardt. Basel: Schwabe & Co., Verlag, 1949–63.

Condorcet, Marquis de, "Discours sur les conventions nationales" (April 1, 1791), in *Oeuvres,* vol. 16.

Condorcet, Marquis de, "Rede über Monarchie und Republik" (1791), in *Oeuvres,* vols. 11 and 13.

Condorcet, Marquis de, *Oeuvres completes,* 21 vols., ed. M. L. S. Cavitat. Brunswick & Paris: Vieweg & Heinrichs, 1804.

Bibliography to the 1926 Edition

Donoso-Cortés, Juan, "Ensayo sobre el Catolicismo, el Liberalismo y el Socialismo," in *Obras de Don Juan Donoso-Cortés*, 10 vols. Madrid: Tejado, 1854–55.

Duguit, Leon, and Henry Monnier, *Les Constitutions et les principales lois politiques de la France depuis 1789*. Paris: Librairie Générale de Droit et de Jurisprudence, 1915 (3d edition).

Esmein, Adhémar, *Éléments de droit constitutionnel*. Paris: Librairie de la Société du Recueil Général des Lois et des Arrets, 1909 (5th edition).

Esmein, Adhémar, and F. Nezard, *Éléments de droit constitutionnel*. Paris: Sirey, 1921.

Ferri, Enrico, *Die revolutionäre Methode*. Leipzig: Hirschfeld, 1907–10. (Translated with an introduction by Robert Michels in the series, Hauptwerke des Socialismus und der Sozialpolitik.)

Figgis, John Neville, *The Divine Right of Kings*. Cambridge: Cambridge University Press, 1914 (2d edition).

Forçade, Eugene, "L'Historien et l'Heroes," in *Études historiques* (Paris: Michael Levy, 1853), 1–43.

Gerber, Emil, "Über den Begriff der Representation in der deutschen Literatur, 1815–1848." Ph.D. diss., Bonn, 1926.

Göppert, Heinrich, *Staat und Wirtschaft*. Tübingen: Mohr, 1924.

Grotius, *De jure belli ac Pacis*. 1631.

Guizot, François Pierre Guillaume, *Histoire des origines du gouvernement représentatif en France*, 2 vols. Paris: Didier, 1851.

Gumplowicz, Ludwig, *Soziologie und Politik*. Leipzig: Duncker & Humblot, 1892.

Guyot, Yves, *Politique Parlamentaire—Politique Atavique*. Paris: Felix Alcan, 1924.

Hamilton, Alexander, *The Federalist Papers*. No. 70, March 18, 1788.

Hasbach, Wilhelm, "Gewaltenteilung, Gewaltentrennung und gemischte Staatsform." *Vierteljahrsschrift für Sozial und Wirtschaftsgeschichte*, 13 (1916), 562–607.

Hasbach, Wilhelm, *Die moderne Demokratie. Eine politische Beschreibung*. Jena: Verlag von Gustav Fischer, 1913, 1921.

Hasbach, Wilhelm, *Die parlamentarische Kabinettsregierung ausserhalb England*. Stuttgart: Deutsche Verlags Anstalt, 1919.

Hauriou, Maurice, *Précis de droit administratif et de droit public*. Paris: Recueil Sirey, 1914.

Bibliography to the 1926 Edition

Hauriou, Maurice, *Précis élémentaire de droit constitutionnel.* Paris: Recueil Sirey, 1923.

Hefele, Hermann, "Demokratie und Liberalismus." *Hochland,* 22 (1924–25), 34–43.

Hegel, G. W. F., *Enzyklopädie.* Berlin: L. Heimann, 1870.

Hegel, G. W. F., *Grundlinien der Philosophie des Rechtsphilosophie.* 1821.

Herrfahrdt, Heinrich, *Das Problem der berufsständischen Vertretung, von den französischen revolution bis zur Gegenwort.* Berlin: Politische Bucherei, 1921.

Hobbes, Thomas, *Leviathan; or, The Matter, Forme and Power of a Commonwealth, Ecclesiastical and Civil.* 1651.

Hugo, Victor, *Napoléon le Petit.* 1852.

Janentzsky, Christian, *J. C. Lavaters "Sturm und Drang" in Zusammenhung seinen religiösen Bewusstseins.* Halle: Neimayer, 1916.

Junius Brutus (pseud.), *Vindiciae contra tyrannos.* 1579.

Kaufmann, Erich, *Kritik der neukantischen Rechtsphilosophie.* Tübingen: Mohr, 1921.

Kaufmann, Erich, *Untersuchungsausschluss und Stattsgerichthof.* Berlin: G. Stelka, 1920.

Kelsen, Hans. *Wesen und Wert der Demokratie.* Tübingen: Mohr, 1921, 1929.

Koellreutter, Otto, *Die Staatslehre Oswald Spenglers. Eine Darstellung und eine kritische Würdigung.* Jena: G. Fischer, 1924.

Krabbe, Hugo, *Die moderne Staatsidee.* The Hague: Martinus Nijhof, 1919.

Lamartine, Alphonse, *Histoire de la Revolution de 1848.* Paris: Penotin, 1848.

Lamartine, Alphonse, *Le Passé, le Présent, l'Avenir de la Republique.* 1848.

Lamartine, Alphonse, *Sur la Politique Rationelle.* Geneva, 1831.

Lambach, W., *Die Herrschaft der 500. Ein Bild des parlamentarischen lebens in Deutschland.* Hamburg: Hanseatische Verlagsanstalt, 1926.

Landauer, Carl, "Die Ideologie des Wirtschaftsparlamentarismus," in Bonn and Payli, *Festgabe für Lujo Brentano,* vol. 1, 153–193.

Landauer, Carl, "Sozialismus und parlamentarisches System." *Archiv für Sozialwissenschaft und Sozialpolitik,* 48 (1922), 748–760.

Landauer, Carl, "Die Wege zur Eroberung des demokratischen Staates durch die Wirtschaftsleiter," in Palyi, ed., *Erinnerungsgabe für Max Weber*, vol. 2. Munich & Leipzig: Duncker & Humblot, 1923, 111–143.

Laski, Harold, *The Foundations of Sovereignty*. New York: Harcourt, Brace & Co., 1921.

Lassalle, Ferdinand, "Herr Bastiat Schulze v. Delitzsch: Der Ökonomische Julian, oder Kapital und Arbeit," in *Gesammelte Reden und Schriften*, 12 vols., ed. E. Bernstein. Berlin: Cassier, 1919.

Lewis, Wyndham, *The Art of Being Ruled*. London: Chatto & Windus, 1922.

Lilburne, John, "Legal Fundamental Liberties of the English People," in *The Clarke Papers*, ed. C. H. Firth. London: The Camden Society, 1794.

Lippmann, Walter, *Public Opinion*. London: George Allen & Unwin, 1922.

Locke, John, *Two Treatises of Government*. 1689.

Löwenstein, Karl, *Minderheitsregierung in Grossbritannien. Verfassungsrechtliche untersuchungen zur neuesten Entwicklungen des britischen Parlamentarismus*. Munich: J. Schweitzer Verlag, 1925.

Löwenstein, Karl, *Volk und Parlament nach der Staatstheorie der französischen Nationalversammlung von 1789. Studien zur dogmengeschichte des unmittlebaren Volksgesetzgebung*. Munich: Drei Masken Verlag, 1922.

Marr, Heinz, "Klasse und Partei in der modernen Demokratie," in *Frankfurter gelehrte Reden und Abhandlungen*, vol. 1. Frankfurt: Englert & Schlofser, 1925.

Marx, Karl, and Friedrich Engels, *Der kommunistische Manifest*. 1848.

Maurras, Charles, *L'avenir de l'intelligence*. Paris: Albert Fontemong, 1905 (2d edition).

Mayer, Otto, *Deutsches Verwaltungsrecht*, 2 vols. Munich & Leipzig: Duncker & Humblot, 1895–96.

Meinecke, Friedrich, *Die Idee der Staatsräson*. Munich & Berlin: Oldenburg, 1924.

Michels, Robert, *Soziologie des Parteiwesens in der modernen Demokratie*. Leipzig: Alfred Kröner Verlag, 1926.

Mohl, Robert von, *Enzyklopädie der Staatswissenschaft*. Tübingen: Laupp'schen Buchhandlung, 1872.

Mohl, Robert von, *Staatsrecht, Völkerrecht und Politik. Monographien*, 3 vols. Tübingen: Verlag der H. Laupp'schen Buchhandlung, 1860–62.

Bibliography to the 1926 Edition

Montesquieu, Baron de, *L'Esprit des lois*. 1748.

Mosca, Gaetano, *Teorica dei governi e Governo Parlamentare*. Milan: Instit. edit. Scientifico, 1925 (2d edition). Rome: Ermanno Loescher, 1884 (1st edition).

Müller-Meiningen, Ernst, *Parlamentarismus. Betrachtungen, Lehren, und Erinnerungen aus deutschen Parlamenten*. Berlin: Walter de Gruyter & Co., 1926.

Murray, Kathleen, *Taine und die englische Romantik*. Munich & Leipzig: Duncker & Humblot, 1924.

Neumann-Hofer, Adolf, "Die Wirksamkeit der Kommissionen in den Parlementen." *Zeitschrift für Politik*, 4 (1911), 51–69.

Ostrogorski, Moisei, *La Démocratie et l'organisation de partis politique*. Paris: Calmann-Lévy, 1903.

Palyi, Melchior, ed., *Hauptprobleme der Soziologie. Erinnerungsgabe für Max Weber*. 2 vols. Munich & Leipzig: Duncker & Humblot, 1922.

Pichler, H., *Zur philosophie der Geschichte*. Tübingen: Mohr, 1922.

Port, Hermann, "Zweiparteiensystem und Zentrum." *Hochland*, 22 (1924–25), 369–377.

Proudhon, Pierre Joseph, "La Guerre et la Paix" (1861), in *Oeuvres complètes*, vols. 13 and 14. Paris: Librairie Internationale, 1867–70.

Pufendorf, Samuel, *De jure naturae et gentium*. 1672.

Redslob, Robert, *Die parlamentarische Regierung in ihrer echten und in ihren unechten Form. Eine vergleichende Studie über die Verfassungen von England, Belgien, Ungarn, Schweden und Frankreich*. Tübingen: Mohr, 1918.

Rosenbaum, Eduard, "Eine Geschichte der Pariser Friedenskonferenz." *Weltwirtschaftliches Archiv*, 18 (1922), 414–424.

Rousseau, Jean-Jacques, *Du contrat social*. 1762.

Schmitt, Carl, "Der Begriff der modernen Demokratie in seinem Verhältnis zum Staatsbegriff." *Archiv für Sozialwissenschaft und Sozialpolitik*, 51 (1924), 817–823.

Schmitt, Carl, "Zu Friedrich Meinecke's *Idee der Staatsräson*." *Archiv für Sozialwissenschaft und Sozialpolitik*, 56 (1926), 226–234.

Schmitt, Carl, *Die Diktatur. Von den Anfängen des modernen Souveränitätsgedankens bis zum proletarischen Klassenkampf*. Munich & Leipzig: Duncker & Humblot, 1921.

Schmitt, Carl, *Die Kernfrage des Völkerbundes*. Berlin: Ferdinand Dümmler, 1926.

Bibliography to the 1926 Edition

Schmitt, Carl, *Politische Romantik*. Munich & Leipzig: Duncker & Humblot, 1919.

Schmitt, Carl, *Politische Theologie. Vier Kapital zur lehre von der Souveränität*. Munich & Leipzig: Duncker & Humblot, 1922.

Sieyès, Emmanuel Joseph Conte, *Politische Schriften*. Leipzig: Gabler'sche Buchhandlung, 1796. (German translation by J. G. Ebel.)

Smend, Rudolf, "Die politische Gewalt im Verfgassungsstaat und das Problem der Staatsform," in *Festgabe für Wilhelm Kahl*. Tübingen: Mohr, 1923.

Smend, Rudolf, "Die Verschiebung der konstitutionellen Ordnung durch Verhältniswahl," in *Festgabe für Karl Bergbohm*, vol. 2. Bonn: A. Marcus & E. Webers, 1919, 278–287.

Sorel, Georges, *Matériaux d'une théorie du prolétariat*. Paris: Marcel Rivière, 1919.

Sorel, Georges, *Réflexions sur la violence*. Paris: Études sur le Devenir social, 1919.

Stein, Lorenz von, *Geschichte der sociale Bewegung im Frankreich von 1789 bis auf unsere Tage*, 3 vols. Leipzig: Wigand, 1850.

Stein, Lorenz von, *Der Socialismus und Communismus des heutigen Frankreichs. Ein Beitrag zur Zeitgeschichte*. Leipzig: Wigand, 1848.

Stein, Lorenz von. *Die Socialistischen und communistischen Bewegungen, 1848*. Leipzig: Wigand, 1850.

Tatarin-Tarnheyden, Edgar, "Kopfzahldemokratie: Organische Demokratie und Oberhausproblem." *Zeitschrift für Politik*, 15 (1926), 97–122.

Tatarin-Tarnheyden, Edgar, *Die Berufsstände, ihre Stellung im Staatsrecht und die deutsche Wirtschaftsverfassung*. Berlin: Carl Heymann, 1922.

Thoma, Richard, "Der Begriff der modernen Demokratie in seinem Verhältnis zum Staatsbegriff," in Palyi, ed., *Erinnerungsgabe für Max Weber*, vol. 2. Munich & Leipzig: Duncker & Humblot, 1922, 37–64.

Thoma, Richard, "Zur Ideologie des Parlamentarismus und der Diktatur." *Archiv für Sozialwissenschaft und Sozialpolitik*, 53 (1924), 212–217.

Tönnies, F., *Kritik der öffentliche Meinung*. Berlin: Springer, 1922.

Weber, Alfred, *Die Krise des modernen Staatsgedankens in Europa*. Stuttgart: Deutsche Verlags Anstalt, 1925.

Bibliography to the 1926 Edition

Weber, Max, "Parlament und Regierung im neugeordneten Deutschland." *Frankfurter Zeitung*, May 1918.

Zitelmann, Ernst, *Irrtum und Rechtsgeschäft*. Leipzig: Duncker & Humblot, 1879.

Zweig, Egon, *Die Lehre vom pouvoir constituant*. Tübingen: Mohr, 1909.

Bibliographical Note

Although there is a large literature on Carl Schmitt's political theory in German and other European languages, relatively little has been published in English on his thought, and until the translations in this series appeared, only *Der Begriff des Politischen* (translated with notes and an introduction by George Schwab as *The Concept of the Political*) was currently available. For those wishing to study his ideas and life, there are two major sources in English: George Schwab's *The Challenge of the Exception: An Introduction to the Political Ideas of Carl Schmitt between 1921 and 1936* (1970) and Joseph Bendersky's *Carl Schmitt: Theorist for the Reich* (1983). Both Schwab and Bendersky have also written important articles on aspects of Schmitt's theory and life. Joseph Bendersky's articles include "Carl Schmitt Confronts the English-speaking World," *Canadian Journal of Political and Social Theory/Revue canadienne de theorie politique et sociale*, 2 (1978), 125–135; "Carl Schmitt in the Summer of 1932: A Reexamination," *Cahiers Vilfredo Pareto: Revue européenne des sciences sociales*, 16 (1978), 39–53; and "The Expendable *Kronjurist*: Carl Schmitt and National Socialism, 1933–1936," *Journal of Contemporary History*, 14 (1979), 309–328. The intense controversy that surrounds Schmitt is conveyed by George Schwab's "Carl Schmitt: Political Opportunist?", *Intellect Magazine*, 103 (1974), 334–337. Schwab's "Schmitt Scholarship," *Canadian Journal of Political and Social Theory/Revue canadienne de theorie politique et sociale*, 4 (1980), 149–155, describes the obstacles to an assessment of Schmitt's theory that the author found in postwar America. In "Carl Schmitt in West German Perspective," *West European Politics*, 4 (1984), 120–127, I have reviewed the Germans' attitudes toward Carl Schmitt during the postwar period. Charles E. Frye, "Carl Schmitt's Concept of the Political," *Journal of Politics*, 28 (1966), 818–830, offers an instructive example of how Schmitt's work has generally been read in America since 1945, and F. R. Cristi's "Hayek and Schmitt on the Rule of Law," *Canadian Journal of Political Science*, 17:3 (1984), 521–535, indicates something perhaps of the interest Schmitt's thought has for a younger generation of scholars.

Despite a growing interest in Schmitt's work, there is very little in English on the political thought of the Weimar Republic in general. Contemporary historians tend either to ignore constitutional and political theory in favor of German social history or, more rarely now, to write history as the story of "great men" and the description of culture. Volker Berghahn's otherwise excellent *Modern Germany* (1982), for example, devotes a considerable amount of space to parliamentarism, but does not even refer to Schmitt and the theorists discussed in the introduction to this book. Gordon Craig, by contrast, mentions Schmitt only as an example in the highly descriptive chapter on German intellectuals in his *Germany: 1866–1945* (Oxford: Oxford University Press, 1980). Until some correlation of all these approaches—theoretical analysis, social history, and political history—is attempted, English scholarship is likely to remain only a fragmented picture of the German past. I have tried to do this in "The Politics of Toleration in Late Weimar: Hermann Heller's Analysis of Fascism and Political Culture," *History of Political Thought*, 5 (1984), 109–127. Keith Tribe's translations of Max Weber, Franz Neumann, and Otto Kirchheimer, and his very useful introductions to their work, which have appeared in the journal *Economy and Society* since 1981, have also helped to make German politics and theory in the Weimar Republic more accessible to an English-speaking audience. Wilhelm Hennis's article "Max Weber's Central Question," *Economy and Society*, 12 (1983), 135–180, is an example of the new reading of German political thought that places it in its historical context, without suffocating the tension and intellectual excitement of the Germans' predicament in this century.

As an introduction to German constitutional politics, Martin Brozat's *Der Staat Hitlers: Grundlegung und Entwicklung seiner inneren Verfassung*, now available in English as *The Hitler State* (London: Longmans, 1981), is to be recommended. But a comparable work on the Weimar Republic and *Kaiserreich* is not available, and there is currently no general introduction in English to German political thought in the period from 1848 to 1945. For students with German, a huge literature exists on Schmitt and his contemporaries. This and Schmitt's own publications have been painstakingly catalogued by Piet Tommissen in his bibliographies: "Carl-Schmitt-Bibliographie," in *Festschrift für Carl Schmitt zum 70. Geburtstag*, ed. Hans Barion et al. (Berlin: Duncker & Humblot, 1959); "Ergänzungsliste zur Carl-Schmitt Bibliographie vom Jahre 1959," in *Epirrhosis: Festgabe für Carl Schmitt*, ed. Hans Barion et al. (Berlin: Duncker & Humblot, 1968), 2 vols.; and "Zweite Fortsetzungsliste der C.S.-Bibliographie vom Jahre 1959," *Cahiers Vilfredo Pareto: Revue européenne des sciences sociales*, 16 (1978), 187–238.

Index

Index